Young Writers 2005 POETRY COMPETITION

Playground Poets

Let your creativity flow...

CW00606277

Eastern Counties

Edited by Lynsey Hawkins

 Young**Writers**

First published in Great Britain in 2005 by:
Young Writers
Remus House
Coltsfoot Drive
Peterborough
PE2 9JX
Telephone: 01733 890066
Website: www.youngwriters.co.uk

SB ISBN 1 84602 105 7

Foreword

Young Writers was established in 1991 and has been passionately devoted to the promotion of reading and writing in children and young adults ever since. The quest continues today. Young Writers remains as committed to the fostering of burgeoning poetic and literary talent as ever.

This year's Young Writers competition has proven as vibrant and dynamic as ever and we are delighted to present a showcase of the best poetry from across the UK. Each poem has been carefully selected from a wealth of *Playground Poets* entries before ultimately being published in this, our thirteenth primary school poetry series.

Once again, we have been supremely impressed by the overall high quality of the entries we have received. The imagination, energy and creativity which has gone into each young writer's entry made choosing the best poems a challenging and often difficult but ultimately hugely rewarding task - the general high standard of the work submitted amply vindicating this opportunity to bring their poetry to a larger appreciative audience.

We sincerely hope you are pleased with our final selection and that you will enjoy *Playground Poets Eastern Counties* for many years to come.

Contents

Beehive Preparatory School, Ilford

Benyon Primary School, South Ockendon

Bildeston Primary School, Ipswich

Lindsey Brown (10)	46
Natalie Squirrell (10)	47
Alex Powell Davies (11)	47
Alice Oxford (11)	47
Liam Chinery (11)	48
James Bateson (11)	48
Sophie Hooper (11)	48
Kerie Breeze (11)	49
Sophie Brinkley (11)	49
Philip Shirley (10)	49
Charlotte Crust (10)	50
Joel Sherwin (10)	51
Paige Lynn (10)	51
Charles Lester (10)	52
Samuel Taylor (11)	52
Brent Walker (10)	53
Martin Greenacre (10)	53
Jamie Ashworth (10)	54
Kitty Rodwell (10)	54

Cherry Trees School, Bury St Edmunds

Helena McColl (10)	55

Darlinghurst Primary School, Leigh-on-Sea

Sophie Linnett (9)	56
Saffron Joiner (9)	57
Kymberlee Webb (9)	57
Michael Goose (8)	58
Rebecca Kibria (10)	58
Harmony Brandon (9)	59
Leah-May Keeble (10)	59
Joe Arber (10) & Theo Brown (9)	60
Morgan Court (8)	60
Jamie Reed (9)	61
Jordaná Fooks (10)	61
Emily Barnes (9)	62
Kirsty Pennycook (10)	62
Ashley Horsburgh (10)	63
Shamima Hussain (9)	63

Sophie Wade (10)	64
Rebecca Davis (10)	64
Jack Burns (10)	65
Reece Farrugia (9)	65
Chloè Gyamfi (10)	66
Gemma Andrews (8)	66
Zoe Angus (9)	67
Susanna Kadur (9)	67
Dannielle Cohen (8)	68
Jack Kerry (9)	68
Zoë Newton (9)	69
William Medhurst (8)	69
Andrew Livett (9)	70
Cy Daly (8)	70
Tara King (9)	71
Helen Archer (8)	71
Jade Hall (8)	71
Robyn Walton (8)	72
Aidan Romero Muñoz (8)	72
Gauge Salter (9)	72
Shannon Willson (9)	73
Ella Dakin (8)	73
George Haley (9)	73
Billy Blewitt (10)	74

Godwin Primary School, Dagenham

Danielle Barwick (10)	74
Abigail Parker (10)	75
Hannah Stanley (10)	75
Sara Rayment (10)	75
Victoria Heed (10)	76

Gunthorpe Primary School, Peterborough

Connor Jackson (10)	76
Emma Sansom (9)	76
Lauren Maloney (10)	77
Sophie Emery (9)	77
Jack Dolby (9)	77
Georgia Calver (9)	78
Ranasha Lotmore (9)	78
Emma Holman (9)	78

Karina Mayes (9)	79
Shona Warren (9)	79
Joel Grenfell (10)	79
Paige Cann (9)	80
Chelsey Etherington (9)	80
Amy Clipston (9)	80
Adam Lomas (10)	81
Nicola Anderson (9)	81
Scott Sherriff (9)	82
Jade Lowbridge (9)	82

Holy Trinity CE Primary School, Colchester

Rachael Bartlett (10)	83
Charlotte Peck (11)	84
Jack Gatland (10)	85
Holly Garwood (10)	86
Isobel Scott (10)	87
Emily Balls (9)	88
Holly Morgan (10)	89
Samantha Payne (11)	90
James Bowles (10)	91
Carl Hollingshead (10)	92
Hazel King (10)	93
Rebecca Herbert (10)	94
Rachael Weighill (10)	94
Jordan Lateward (11)	95
Annabelle Matthews (10)	95
Hayley Kelsey (11)	96
Kyle Smith (10)	97
Gemma Dove (11)	97
Alex Cronin (11)	98
Becky Davies (11)	98
Katie O'Brien (10)	99

Lee Chapel Primary School, Basildon

Brooke Saunders (9)	99

Mayfield Primary School, Cambridge

Tom Harvey (8)	100
Joseph Harvey (8)	100

Benjamin Winger (9)	101
Oliver Dawes (9)	101
Phoebe Bostock (8)	102
Sophie Tullett (8)	102
Soo-Suk Lee (8)	103
Mara Pintilie (9)	104
Alex Cosme (8)	105
Connie Kim (9)	106
Fleur Watson (9)	107
Robin Macdonald (9)	108
Neha Aggarwal (8)	109
Alice Hembrow (8)	110
Francesca Morelli (8)	111

Monks Risborough CE School, Princes Risborough

Lauren Roads (10)	111
Dominic Pavlopoulos (9)	112
Thomas Lidington (9)	112
Amy Lipyeart (9)	113
Sean Hinton (9)	113
Charlie Walker (10)	114
Matthew Zelmanowicz (9)	114
Danielle Rolfe (9)	115
Jamie-Lee Brooker (10)	115
Coral Morgan (10)	115
James Myerson (9)	116
George Moran (9)	116
Oliver Kamperis (10)	116
Sarah Smart (10)	117
Emily Brundrett (10)	118
Marcus Nielsen (10)	119
Barnaby Matthews (9)	120
Conor Walker (9)	120

Oak Green School, Aylesbury

Lukmaan Jabar (10)	121
Desmond Mujana (9)	121
Sarfaraz Saghir (10)	121
Lauren Byrne (9)	122
Tabassum Naeem (9)	122
Hallid Mahmood (9)	122

Tyler May (9)	123
Holly Revell (10)	123
Haroon Humzah (10)	123
Georgia Crane (9)	124
Morgan McCarthy (8)	124
Connor Hennigan (7)	124
Luke Bright (9)	125
Kathryn Dixon (8)	125
Jasmine Street (8)	125
Rikki Jones (9)	126
Joe Craig (9)	126
Danielle Webb (8)	126
Daltan Taylor (9)	127
Rheanne Gordon (9)	127
Callum Jones (9)	127
Billy Rogers (9)	128
Paige Stevenson (8)	128
Macauley Stott (9)	128
Georgia Adams (8)	129
Elliot Riley (8)	129
Shannon Woolhead (8)	129
Alisha Bruno (8)	130
Courtney Green (9)	130
William Ginn (9)	130
Megan Brown (8)	131
Otis Roberts (9)	131
Lucy Sprowell (8)	131
Nazish Abbas (9)	132
Rafael Rebelo-Miranda (9)	132
KC Franceschini (9)	132
Amber Nasreen (9)	133
Abbie Osborne (9)	133
Ieva Pakalniskyte (9)	133
Chelsea Davies (9)	134
Jade Street (8)	134
Mohammed Aftab (9)	134
Amber Whitney (9)	135
Lucy Warwick (9)	135
Leah Clayton-Temple (9)	135
Hannah Baldwin (9)	136

Priory School, Prittlewell

Luke Murphy (10)	136
Jordan Needs (10)	136

St Helen's Primary School, Ipswich

Owen Rees (9)	137
Louie Bloom (8)	137
Francesca Cross (9)	138
Pratik Bikkannavar (9)	138
Carlie Osborne (8)	139
Afsana Islam (11)	139
Ottillie Cook (8)	140
Tiffany Evripidou (8)	140
Yiuk-Ngor To (8)	141
Isabella Carrino (9)	142
Emily Clarke-Beard (10)	142
Beckie Fiddaman (9)	143
Ellie Goodwin (9)	143
Jacob Buckley (9)	144
Thomas Powell (9)	144
Jake Templeton (8)	145
Stacey Walker (9)	145
Bethany Durrant (9)	146
Brennan Butler (11)	146
Tanatswa Kazangarare (9)	147
Paul Armitage (7)	147
Tansie Shoults (7)	147
Hannie Phillips (8)	148
Maggie Fielder (10)	148
Hannah Turner (9)	149
Kelsie Simmons (10)	149
Soham Dixit (9)	150
Imogen Milner (8)	150
Amelia Cousins (10)	151
Josef Bryant (7)	151
Matthew Gerrard (10)	152
Tom Warburton (7)	152
Katie Pettican (10)	153
Iqbal Ali (9)	153
Rhys Lucock (10)	154
Jemima Hindmarch (8)	154

Spinfield School, Marlow

Sophie Natynczyk (10)   191
Katie Green (10)   191
Jack Wheeler (10)   192
Jack Smith (10)   192

West Walton Community Primary School, Wisbech
Oskar Thomas (10)   193
Callum Pitcher (11)   193
Charlotte Sear (11)   194
Caitlin Thorpe (10)   194
James Gifford (10)   195
Lorna Deller (10)   195
Laura Tilney (10)   196
Maise Hunns (11)   196
Christopher Vick (10)   197
Kelsey McKenna (10)   197
Emma Rogers (10)   198
Sam Melton (10)   199
Paul Whyatt (11)   199
Alice Edwards (11)   200
Bethany Brightey (10)   200
Jonathan Thompson (10)   201
Bethany Smith (11)   201
Aaron Gosling (11)   202
Liam Follen (10)   202
James Brazil (10)   203
Rebecca Crane (11)   203
Nicole Young (10)   203
Robert Brooks (10)   204

The Poems

Raindrop

I am a blue crystal from your ring
And I turn to ice when it's freezing
I come out night and day
To come out and play
When there's a puddle
I fall down from the sky and make a *splash!*
I am a raindrop from the clouds!

Francine Cozzetto (8)

Happiness

Happiness is like daffodils dancing in the sun
It sounds like birds singing from the sky
It tastes like sweet sugar being shoved down your throat
It looks like the blue sky
It feels like cuddling into my big toy dog
It reminds me of playing in the school with my friends.

Ashley Bragg (9)

Maths Lessons

(To the rhythm of Mary Mary)

Digits, digits,
Make me fidget,
That's how maths lessons go.
With tiny fractions
And large subtractions
And averages all in a row!

Aaron Naisbitt (11)
Bancroft's Preparatory School, Woodford Green

On We Go To War

A camouflage of green and grey,
My boots are thick and heavy,
The gun that I carry weighs me down,
As I wave goodbye.

A single tear runs down my cheek,
Not a smile on my love's face,
My children cling to my legs,
As I wave goodbye.

France is where we have to be,
A necessity against the Nazis,
I tell my family once again,
As I wave goodbye.

My face pressed hard against the window,
A kiss blown at my beloved wife,
I stiffly stare as the train starts moving,
Goodbye, goodbye, goodbye.

Alison Harvey (11)
Bancroft's Preparatory School, Woodford Green

Evacuation

When I was at school one day,
All the noise seemed to go like water goes down a drain.
The teacher came out and my blood froze.
It was now the time to leave my family.
My heart wept and wept.
We walked slowly and no sound seemed to emerge.
Everyone knew what was happening.
The time we were at the station,
We go into the train and sat down.
The soft padding of the seats tried to comfort me,
But it was no use because I was still sad.
The train left and the beat of the train soothed me to sleep.

Adán Mordcovich (11)
Bancroft's Preparatory School, Woodford Green

The Rainforest

Entering the world of harmonic melodies
Birds basking in the powerful rays of the sun
Their unique voices roam the air
And drown out any sorrow

Beetles toil under a fallen branch
Pure water carving its identity on the rich soil
Leaves praying towards the glorious sun

This bliss
This happiness
This calmness and tranquillity
This heavenly paradise

Is shattered by the piercing cry of a man
A snake leaves the scene
Beads of sweat trickle down the pale face of fear
He gazes vacantly at the dancing shadows from under the canopy . . .

Gheed Mahir (11)
Bancroft's Preparatory School, Woodford Green

The Water Cycle

The sun rises and the heat spreads,
Evaporation forms and the journey begins,
Condensation evolves, clouds are created,
The urging winds pushing it creating storms.

The heavy rains fall to the rivers,
The water flows travelling from meander to meander,
The rivers widen, as the water travels downhill.
The water reaches the mouth and searches its way down to the sea.

The sea opens wide thirsty for more water,
The rivers feed the sea all that it's got,
Is this the end of the journey, or is it once again the beginning?

Salisha Amin (11)
Bancroft's Preparatory School, Woodford Green

The Raindrop

It started as a raindrop,
Falling from a cloud,
It hit the dusty mountainside
And began to swirl and glide.
Getting bigger every minute,
Now a stream appears,
Gathering speed, it twists and turns,
Now in sight the waterfall;
Crashing down in a thunderous torrent,
On jagged rocks below,
Fish darting to and fro.
Rushes dotted here and there,
Coffee-brown in colour,
The sight is calming to the eye
And so it calms the river.

Neha Agarwala (10)
Bancroft's Preparatory School, Woodford Green

Tulips

Tulips swaying in the breeze,
Red, orange, yellow.
Holding their heads up high,
White, lilac, peach.

Never a care in the world,
Amber, scarlet, crimson.
Forever stuck to the ground,
Blue, violet, purple.

Slowly fading away,
Plum, cream, navy.
Gone till next year,
Coral, honeydew, apple.

Stephanie Pinto (11)
Bancroft's Preparatory School, Woodford Green

World War II

Barrage balloons explode.
Aircraft engine's whirling stops.
Shattered metal drops.

Black-crossed Nazi planes,
Dodging through the searchlight's range,
Air raid sirens change.

Rising, falling beat.
Hearts are pounding stirred by fear,
Swaying in the wind.

Black sky; men falling.
White silk mushrooms opening,
Swaying in the wind.

Startled babies screaming,
Mothers running from their work,
Fears in ditches lurk.

Barbed wire coiled beach,
Anti-aircraft blazing guns,
Winston Churchill's speech.

Blue, stiff-legged bodies.
Blood-splattered fields. Now poppies.
Hoping, fearing, *death*.

Kush Sikka (10)
Bancroft's Preparatory School, Woodford Green

An Evacuee's Train Ride

I'm on the train, there's no going back,
The train is moving on the railway track.

Half choking on steam, half choking on tears,
How jerkily the driver steers.

I'm pushed and I'm shoved and thrown about,
I'm going to be lonely, without a doubt.

We're drawing away from Mum and Dad,
Should I be feeling so terribly sad?

This seat is uncomfortable, the scenery is poor,
Inconsiderate people shove and push, now I'm on the hard, cold floor.

Stamped on and flattened out is not my first choice,
I kick and I scream, I strain my voice.

I see a tree, I see a beach!
What other surprise could we possibly reach?

It won't be so bad after all,
So I'll be happy and stand up tall.

Lydia Katsis (11)
Bancroft's Preparatory School, Woodford Green

Choices, Choices

I'm considering a Flake,
But caramel is nice,
Or should it be Cadbury Marble,
Or those dainty chocolate mice?
For pudding I think I may have Twix,
Or maybe Milky Way,
But now I come to think of it,
I'll have a pick 'n' mix,
A KitKat would be tasty,
Or a Crunchie even better,
I think I'd betta getta . . .
Galaxy!

Elena Markovitch (10)
Bancroft's Preparatory School, Woodford Green

Young Writers - Playground Poets Eastern Counties

Tsunami

I raged out of the sea,
Bringing a series of deadly waves.
Hitting shores as I spread my wings,
From country to country.

But I didn't harm anyone,
So I ebbed back disappointed.
As I receded,
I heard laughter, 'Ha-ha, you can't harm a fly!'

So I went back again.

I come at the speed of lightning,
Slamming villages and tourists,
Destroying roads and houses,
From country to country.

I dragged people out to sea,
Tearing families apart
And drowning everything on my way,
From country to country.

I come with overwhelming force,
Ripping trains from the tracks,
Turning buildings to rubble,
From country to country.

Neville Jacob (10)
Bancroft's Preparatory School, Woodford Green

My Poem

Poems, poems,
paper and ink.

Poems, poems,
boring old things!

Poems, poems,
make them rhyme.

Poems, poems,
line by line.

Poems, poems,
I wrote one for school.

Poems, poems,
I don't think they're cool!

Some about cats,
some about dogs.

Some about boots,
some about clogs.

Mine's about poems,
yes, them again!

Poems, poems, poems . . .

Where's my pen?

Katherlne Stevens (10)
Bancroft's Preparatory School, Woodford Green

Boy Without Friends

Why do people not care about me?
Is it what I do?
Is it what I see?
Would it be my creed or colour
Or something else that doesn't matter?

I want somebody to talk to,
A girl or a boy,
I've even been through therapy,
But nothing fills the void.

On a hot summer's day,
I'm on a bench in the park,
All the ducks swim away,
Then the light dims, and it grows dark.

Alone on my bed,
Sadly I lie,
I want happiness and friends,
But none come my way.

I've got something to say,
'I just want some friends.'
And that is the message
That I'd like to send

And now as I leave you,
I know you might laugh,
But just think about me, with a life of misery,
When you're alone in the dark.

Callum Mehta   (10)
Bancroft's Preparatory School, Woodford Green

Lion

Lions prowl around the jungle,
Hoping to find their prey.
They are sly, suspicious and sceptical,
Get in their way at your peril.

Their paws pad gently on the ground,
Their noses sniff into the air,
Their ears are as sharp as razors,
Their teeth are fangs like Dracula's!

They search high; they look into the trees,
They search low; they look into the caves,
To find some meat,
To satisfy their rumbling tums.

They hear a sound, they see it move,
They crouch down low,
They stretch their jaws . . .
It looks like a cruel smile.

The gazelle prances around the bush,
Acting like royalty, unsuspecting of anything.
The lion gives no warning,
He jumps up high, his mane swaying and then he . . .
Pounces!

Elizabeth Ogundiya (9)
Bancroft's Preparatory School, Woodford Green

Homeless

I fear this year will be my last.
The streets are silent.
I have trudged miles from my last home.
I want to flee from my deathbed.
My feet are numb.
The biting winds seep through to my bones.

I walk past a pub.
Someone throws a glass.
I yell and fall to the ground.
People see and start laughing.

I limp towards a lake of black water.
A rat scurries away from me.
A small boy with his mum drops a bag of Hovis bread.
The ducks quack noisily.
He bends down to pick it up.
'It's dirty, leave it!' shouts his mother.
She drags him away.

When you're a tramp
Nobody wants you.

Richie Layburn (10)
Bancroft's Preparatory School, Woodford Green

Bullies

When the bullies come
My knees start to shake
When the bullies come
My body starts to quake

When the bullies come
My sweat starts to pour
When the bullies come
My heart starts to roar

When the bullies come
My fingers start to tremble
When the bullies come
My stomach starts to rumble

When the bullies come
My eyes start to water
When the bullies come
My strength starts to falter

When the bullies come
Run!

Rory Strycharczyk (10)
Bancroft's Preparatory School, Woodford Green

Wild Or Tame?

Creeping, creeping . . .
I creep through the grass like a snake over sand
I jump
Missed!
Skimming through the grass like a fish through water
I pounce
Missed once more
I pause to lick my dark, dusty coat
Big mistake
Something leaps at my back
I turn as best I can . . .
And shake loose
I don't like foreign cats in my territory (as you can see)
You may not think I'm much good at hunting
But when it comes to my home and territory
Well . . .

Sarah Wright (10)
Bancroft's Preparatory School, Woodford Green

Spring And Winter

Flowers bursting open, revealing all their beauty,
Blossom blooming pink and white on the bare trees.
Ponds covered with ice freezing all the water,
Icicles hanging from branches ready to drop.

Pretty coloured flowers, red, orange, blue and pink,
Lots of yellow daffodils swinging in slight breezes.
Snow falling heavily, blocking up the roads,
Children making snowmen, wearing hats and gloves.

New sounds coming to the world of creatures being born.
It is the season of beauty and baby animals starting their life.
People start decorating for the event of Christmas,
Swapping lots of presents full of lovely toys.

Emily Nickerson (11)
Bancroft's Preparatory School, Woodford Green

Dinner Ladies

Dinner ladies are vile and cruel,
they feed you the worst food,
they shout at us and threaten us
and think we're rude!

Many children walk home with terrible tummy bugs,
they don't even care,
they think we're the biggest moaners,
but we're just scared.

It's 11 o'clock, dreaded hour of the day,
most children like lunchtime,
but we'd rather stay away.
We dread the pop when the dinner lady's spots explode,
still some lurking around!

The tolling bell almost here to take us to our illness.
Sometimes we think of running out of the school to freedom,
but those are only fantasies,
reality is waiting in line for *gruel!*

As the teachers sit down to eat a plump roast turkey
on beautiful red velvet chairs,
we sit down on almost-broken wooden chairs
and listen to the eerie scratching sound of the trays
and the metal canteen,
eating something that's meant to be sausages and beans!

Children are starting to run out the room
to be sick in their reservational toilet,
I doubt a lot that the toilets will smell nice and fragrant,
the toilets aren't far away so you can hear the heaving of
every single child.

I've almost finished all my food, which is one of the rules,
I also feel sick.
I'm glad my cubicle awaits me and
oh no, I'm going to be - 'Errhh!'

Eloise Marché (9)
Bancroft's Preparatory School, Woodford Green

Hungry Cat

I wake up and stretch,
What a rude awakening! I'm practically thrown out of bed!
I have no choice but to jump off. It's better than being thrown off!
My senses lead me to the kitchen. Mmmm!
I pad across the shiny floor. Great! I didn't skid!
The sun glares through the dirty window. Hmm. Is that food
                                        I see out there?
I want to catch it so badly, but that means I have to squeeze
                                        through that tiny door,
It leaves me so sore, but I'm so hungry, *squeeze.*
The prey is innocently burying its food. Yet it's not innocent
                                        enough for me!
Too late. It ran away. I'll find something else for today.
I squeeze back into the kitchen - its smell has gone.
Yet the living room has gained one!
I run, and skid this time.
I see the man who always feeds me (but not now unfortunately!)
More importantly, I see his food!
I jump up and I'm sucked into the great big leather whirlpool
                                        of the sofa.

Once I've waded across, I suddenly get shoved off.
I stick my tail in the air and sulk off into the kitchen.
Why should I care? But I do - he has food!
I pad into the kitchen and I see *my* food!
It's fatty and greasy; it's just not fair.
His food is nicer, but I don't care!
So I gobble it up as I realise I'm . . . *hungry!*

Holly Carter (10)
Bancroft's Preparatory School, Woodford Green

The Storm

The first wave of the storm,
Crashed against our boat.
It hurled the craft around,
But we still stayed afloat.

The waves had drenched our clothes,
The salt made our eyes sting.
What had caused the storm?
It could be anything.

Lighting from the clouds,
Burst across the night,
The thunder all around me,
Rumbled with all its might.

The wind howled in my ears
And pushed back all my hair.
The storm was like a beast,
Who'd just escaped his lair.

Charles Blake (9)
Bancroft's Preparatory School, Woodford Green

Stormy Weather

S torm a-brewing
T errifying
O cean swirling
R ain lashing
M ast swinging
Y ells for help

W ater gushing
E lectrifying lightning
A iry atmosphere
T hunder cracking
H arbour lights are dim
E verything clearing
R ight again.

Chloé Michaud (10)
Bancroft's Preparatory School, Woodford Green

The Playground

I could see boys playing football,
Shouting and sweating as they did it,
I could see girls skipping and laughing as they did it,
Both things looked such fun; I wish I could join in.
I could hear boys calling, *'Goal!'* or *'Yes!'*
I could see girls gossiping saying, 'Hey, did you know that . . . ?'
It looked such fun, I wish I could join in.

I could hear girls laughing and talking happily,
I could hear boys calling out, 'Our team won!'
I could hear boys arguing that they got the point,
It looked so much fun, I wish I could join in.
It's as though I'm a lame rabbit,
That nobody can see.
Everybody hates me!

Leah Fisher (10)
Bancroft's Preparatory School, Woodford Green

The Storm

On a boat in the stormy sea,
Crashing waves, screeching wind.
Yelling, 'Take in the sails.'
'Hurry, hurry!' I yell. 'Please, quick.'
The storm like a roaring lion,
Hard like a chair,
Freezing, bleak.
Black clouds swirling, raging.
Harsh black-blue sea.
The ship's hit the rock,
'Quick cover the hole,' I screech.
Nearer the water,
In the water,
Bubbles on the surface,
Dead.

Lucy Gatrell (9)
Bancroft's Preparatory School, Woodford Green

Playground Cares

Nobody cares,
All I can see,
Girls gossiping,
Skipping
And footballs hurtling into goals,
Nobody cares about poor old me.

Nobody cares,
All I can hear being said,
'Goal!'
And 'High five man!'
Nobody talks to me 'cause
Nobody cares about poor old me.

Nobody cares,
All I can taste,
Is the air and blood,
As a ball hit me,
Not even 'sorry', 'cause,
Nobody cares about poor old me.

Nobody cares,
All I can hear,
Girls giggling,
Shouting
And balls being kicked,
No voices to talk to me 'cause,
Nobody cares about poor old me.

And all I keep thinking is,
What is the use of playground games?

Ciara Murphy (9)
Bancroft's Preparatory School, Woodford Green

The Mingowla

He lives in the darkest realms of the world,
In caves deep in the mountains,
Eyes of fire has the Mingowla
And wings as rough as the coarsest leather.

He soars through the night,
His wings outstretched,
Devouring fruit bats in mid-flight,
Snatching them from the air with his
Great, sharp teeth.

Whacking anything that might get in his way,
With his thick, lumpy tail as he glides,
Like a shadow,
Through the forest.

His ears pricked, alert, waiting for sound,
Perched on a boulder, scanning the view
And then he dives, swooping down on the unsuspecting prey,
His tongue darts out
And a fox is no more.

And then he has had his fill,
So he settles,
Back in the cave, deep in the mountains,
His eyelashes, thick as horse-hair, slowly droop over
                                those deep, dark eyes
And there is silence,
Except for the whispering of rats snuggling into his pink scaly chest,
Just as morning breaks.

Catriona Philip (10)
Bancroft's Preparatory School, Woodford Green

The Playground!

Children
        Skipping
            Jumping
                Running
                     And laughing
                     Playing
                            Football
                  Netball
            And hopscotch

Whoops!
    Shouting
        'Yessss'
            Screaming
                'Oh yeah'
                    Whispering
                    And chattering like a monkey

'Oh yes,' screams a girl
    'Well I went to America . . . boasts another
                'Goal!' screams a boy
                   'Foul!'

Wait a minute where is everybody?
Hmmmmmm . . .
Got to go or I'll be late for class!

Harriet Welton (10)
Bancroft's Preparatory School, Woodford Green

A Noisy Playground

This is a noisy playground,
I can see boys playing football,
Girls skipping,
Playing netball.
This is a noisy playground.
Boys are shouting,
'Hooray!'
'Yes!'
'Goal!'
I can smell the grass being cut.
I can hear shouting,
Laughing,
Whispering,
Talking
And
Cheering.
This is a noisy playground,
But it's not so noisy anymore because
It's time for class!

Abigail Cox (10)
Bancroft's Preparatory School, Woodford Green

Anger

Blood's boiling like a runaway train,
Driving a car, turn right into the fast lane,
Snowing all around me, the black sky falling in.

Might be the drowsiness,
Running through my brain,
I hit the huge truck,
Not even time to duck.

Shackled in chains, my soul feels stained,
Held up in the courtroom,
Charged with having hit a huge truck.

Jordan Doughty (10)
Bancroft's Preparatory School, Woodford Green

The Cruellest Emotion

Anger is tough and very, very strong,
Like a cheetah pouncing on its prey,
It can be ice-cold or as hot as a heatwave,
It can be scarlet-red but sometimes grey.

Wait and wait does the cheetah in the grass,
Stalking and accelerating at amazing speed,
Tearing at its neck it kills the prey,
How tough and how strong that cheetah must be.

The ice melting from Christmas this year,
Brewing into an everlasting heatwave,
The drip, drip, drop of the water comes
From an icicle in a faraway cave.

The scarlet-red is full of rage,
In cheeks full of hatred and fury,
Yet grey is often found in a courtroom,
Through a criminal and witnessed by the jury.

But envy is much more powerful,
A poor man begging for money,
Like an old and rusty car,
Everlasting envy is thicker than honey.

Shout and shout does the beggar,
Wishing there was something in his pocket,
Several coins drop into his bowl,
He hopes that no one will rock it.

The rusty car stands all on its own,
Thoughts rot away with metallic paint,
His thoughts mixed up for the rest of his life,
Stirred in a way that makes him faint.

So which is the cruellest emotion of all?
Is it anger which makes you fight in a brawl
Or envy which makes your mind spin like a ball?

Toby Hunter (11)
Bancroft's Preparatory School, Woodford Green

The Playground Bully

The boys playing football,
Shall I steal the ball?
The girls with their cats' cradles,
Maybe I could pull their string,
Who shall I pick on now?

The girls skipping merrily,
Will that be fun enough?
The boys enjoying playing 'It',
I can easily ruin that,
Who shall I pick on now?

The new boy in the corner,
What a fine choice!
The small girls whispering quietly,
I'll show them a thing or two,
Who shall I pick on now?

But I don't want to pick on anyone,
I just want someone to play with me,
Will you play with me?
Pleeeeeeeeeease!

Miren Radia (10)
Bancroft's Preparatory School, Woodford Green

Sadness

In the cold winter month,
Cooped up inside on the tattered sofa.
Listening to the tear-suggesting music,
The owls outside hoot away.

Feeling miserable and
Looking out into the darkness.
Rain hits the window.
The whole world seems dull and grey.

Harsimran Sanghera (11)
Bancroft's Preparatory School, Woodford Green

The Playground

So here I am in the playground
You know, the usual walk around

Giggling girls, ridiculous boys
And some who even brought their toys

'Goal!' You might hear
Or see someone shedding a tear

Skipping, gossiping, whispering
Teachers ranting and raving

Everyone is enjoying spring
With all the things they have to bring

Everyone's having such fun
But the bell has just rung

End of playtime
I love my precious playtime.

Hazel Ijomah (10)
Bancroft's Preparatory School, Woodford Green

Pride

Pride is a cat
Strutting around with his tail held high.
Acting cool to impress the ladies,
Then runs away at the sight of a dog.

Pride is a pair of leather boots
Glad to be commented on, the centre of attention.
They are not used, just a fashion accessory
And lay untouched on the top of your wardrobe.

Pride is a posh restaurant,
Where the sign outside is flashing bright.
The people all dressed in designer clothes
Having lovely food and expensive wine.

Elizabeth Heard (11)
Bancroft's Preparatory School, Woodford Green

The Moonlight Garden

Outside in the garden
The black panther creeps.
The summer breeze blows
And the stars are asleep.

He stands in the garden,
Proud and tall.
He waits for his mistress,
Her sweet and soft call.

Her eyes draw him nearer
And what he won't miss,
By the light of the moon,
Her soft but sharp kiss.

They can now taste the sweetness
Of all that they share,
Together forever,
They have not a care.

Till morning has come,
Away she must go,
As she sadly slinks
Away in the snow.

Outside in the garden,
The black panther creeps.
The winter wind blows
And the stars stop to sleep.

He stands in the moonlight,
Proud and tall.
He waits for his mistress,
He can't hear her call.

She'll return in the summer,
Fresh and new,
Like a bird that will sing
And a flower that will bloom.

Stephanie Posner (11)
Bancroft's Preparatory School, Woodford Green

A Typical School Trip

'Right everyone, today we're going to visit the Tower of London.
You're going to see lots of exciting things!'

(But first we have to get there.)

'I want all of you to collect one clipboard from the pile,
I said *one* clipboard Caroline, not two.
Put one of your clipboards back, *now!*

Right everyone, follow me.
No, you *cannot* take your Barbie to the Tower of London, Ruby.
Put it back on your desk.

Children, get on the coach,
Not that one! That's a bus!

Say hello to the driver, children,
He's called Mr Enfield,
Smile at him Hilary, don't frown.

Please put your seatbelt on - as soon as you sit down.

Why isn't your seatbelt on Luke?
Don't tell me it was on!
How could it be on if you were talking to Joseph?
He's sitting four rows behind you!

Stop singing at the back,
I said stop singing at the back!
That's better.

What is it now Gideon?
Well why didn't you go before we left school?
Pardon Gideon?
Yes, we're almost there,
Yes, we are almost there!

Mr Enfield,
Are we almost there?'

Linnet Kaymer (10)
Bancroft's Preparatory School, Woodford Green

There's Something In The Corner

There's something in the corner,
It's really dark,
I squeezed my cuddly dog so hard,
It made a little bark.

There's something in the corner,
What could it be?
Is it the Loch Ness monster,
From under the sea?

There's something in the corner,
It smells of bogey-ick,
Yuck! It's getting worse,
I think I'm going to be sick.

There's something in the corner,
I hope it's not the bear from the cave,
I wish Roger was here,
He's my dog who's really brave.

I ran down to my mum's room,
She went to my room with me,
She turned on the light
And this is what I could see.

A scruffy old dog,
That was really smelly,
Its collar said, 'Roger',
I rubbed him on the belly.

So it wasn't the bear or Nessie you see,
It was Roger,
Simple as simple can be.

Provhat Rahman (8)
Bancroft's Preparatory School, Woodford Green

A Soldier In War

I can see blasting bombs in the distance
Fire crackling in the air
Men charging into the night
Planes soaring overhead
While many injured lie dying

I can hear landmines exploding
Soldiers falling to the ground
The sound of screaming amongst the dank smell
And the air force zooming past
But still they fight for their lives

I can feel the tears in my eyes
While men fire their guns
I'm bursting with sadness
My heart's piercing with pain
As my friends die in battle.

Aakash Mayor (8)
Bancroft's Preparatory School, Woodford Green

A Scene Of Love

The white grains of sand trickle through my toes.
Crystal clear waves lap against my feet.
As I look out to sea, a huge ball of fire
Disappears below the horizon.
The glow of the day's heat fades once more.

As I await in the bar, the man of my dreams saunters in.
Our eyes connect across the room
And we gaze at each other.
Memories come flooding back to me,
The love of my past is here again.

We walk back to the beach, hand in hand,
The palm trees wave their leaves in support of our meeting,
There is no need for talk; our eyes say it all.
This time we shall hold onto it forever.

Libby Atherton (10)
Bancroft's Preparatory School, Woodford Green

This Could Be The Death Of You

Flying in a jet plane,
High up in the sky,
War could be the death of you.

Tanks rolling across the ground,
Shooting bullets,
War could be the death of you.

Fire blazing from bombs,
Dropped from jets,
War could be the death of you.

Jets coming from the sky,
Tanks coming from the ground,
War could be the death of you.

Infantry soldiers fighting on the ground,
It's all bad,
War could be the death of you.

Ayrton Ahmet (8)
Bancroft's Preparatory School, Woodford Green

Autumn

The golden leaves are falling
Some are red and brown
The trees are nearly bare now
But summer's just behind

The sound of footsteps in the leaves
The rustling of trees
The raindrops on the rooftops
Are autumn sounds indeed

School is coming back again
It's getting colder now
North wind blowing in my face
With Christmas round the corner.

Ella Young (8)
Bancroft's Preparatory School, Woodford Green

My Dear

I can see the bloody corpses,
mangled by guns and bombs.
Many men are dead,
but I will fight for you my dear,
I will fight for you.

I can hear the screams of death,
from many innocent men.
The songs of war ring in my ears,
but I will fight for you my dear,
I will fight for you.

I can almost taste the blood,
from this war so true,
I can't taste any victory,
but I will fight for you my dear,
I will fight for you.

I feel so pained at the heart,
this bloody war kills too many men.
I'm scared I will die,
but I will fight for you my dear,
I will fight for you.

This war is won,
victory for England!
We ended World War II,
the war is won for you my dear,
the war is won for you.

Nicola Orrell (8)
Bancroft's Preparatory School, Woodford Green

Rain

Dark clouds crowd the sky
Casting shadows as they pass by
The sun is locked away
Nothing glistens, all is grey

Drip, drop, pitter-patter
First a few then a splatter
Tumbling down all around
Then springing up as they hit the ground

Roaring, soaring, plentifully pouring
Dashing, splashing, sliding, gliding
Soaking me from head to toe
No escape, nowhere to go

Then, *plip, plap, plop*
It all comes to a stop.

Clarissa Cameron (9)
Bancroft's Preparatory School, Woodford Green

The River

It came from the source,
With such great force.
This one headed south,
It ended at the mouth.
Tributaries helped it flow,
They were always on the go.
This is my river.

It had rivulets which stole,
Streams of water from its soul.
It meandered on its way,
Passing fields of corn and hay.
The delta spread it wide
And, after that, it died.
This was my river.

Calum Lomas (10)
Bancroft's Preparatory School, Woodford Green

Jealousy

Like a lizard eyeing its prey,
A good, filling dinner who's lost their way.

Like a thunderstorm trying to grab your loved ones and
take them away,
Making sharp, loud comments which will hit you one day,

Like a chipped, crumpled school chair wanting to be
polished like its neighbour,
It is full of sharp, nasty comments and even worse behaviour.

If it goes too far, it can't turn back,
It reminds me of holly-green and ebony-black,

Be it jealousy of money,
Or jealousy of fame,
The end result of jealousy,
Will always be the same!

Happiness is found,
With being peaceful in your life,
Wanting what others want,
Will only cause you strife!

Eleanor Flaherty (10)
Bancroft's Preparatory School, Woodford Green

When I Am An Aeroplane

When I am an aeroplane
I can soar really high,

When I am an aeroplane
I can say bye-bye.

When I am an aeroplane
I can play with the birds,

When I am an aeroplane
I can see loads of herds.

When I am an aeroplane
I can hear people talking,

When I am an aeroplane
I can see people walking.

When I am an aeroplane
I can see the ocean,

When I am an aeroplane
I'll land in slow motion.

Hibah Hafeez (8)
Bancroft's Preparatory School, Woodford Green

Every Morning I Go To The Playground

Every morning I go to the playground,
I play football
And dash around.

Every morning I go to the playground,
I see girls giggling,
While the boys are sniggering.

Every morning I go to the playground,
When it's been raining I jump in a puddle,
That gets my bags in a terrible muddle.

Every morning I go to the playground,
With my Tamagotchi I connect or link,
Then when I run my key rings clink.

Every morning I go to the playground,
I do what I do
And what I do is fun!

Timothy Knott (10)
Bancroft's Preparatory School, Woodford Green

Frustration

Frustration is your homework,
You don't know what to do.
Perhaps you've got a cold
And nothing's getting through.

Frustration is your car,
Lost inside a lot.
You're sitting an exam
And your pen decides to clot.

Frustration is your parents
Always saying no!
If only you were taller,
Then on that ride you'd go.

Frustration is the rain,
You cannot go and play!
You've got the time to fly your kite,
But the sky is always grey.

Simon Russell (11)
Bancroft's Preparatory School, Woodford Green

Sadness

Sadness is a metallic blue shade
And is an emotion where happiness fades,
Sadness likes the heavy rain
And it will bring out all your shame.

Sadness is like an old top hat,
It haunts you inside like a dark black bat,
Sadness is like a flowing river
And it will make your insides shiver.

Sadness comes late in the evening
And it will want to stop you breathing,
Sadness is the winter season
As it comes upon you for no reason.

It feels like you are bound with rope
And is enough to make you mope,
Although this feeling could be absurd,
There is sadness put into words!

Julia McMenemy (10)
Bancroft's Preparatory School, Woodford Green

The Best Season Of The Year

I love summer
It's nice and hot
I get to run around in the garden a lot
I get to play in the pool
And don't have to go to school
I love to eat ice cream
And that's why I love summer a lot.

Aleena Hira Mirza (8)
Beehive Preparatory School, Ilford

I'm A Rock Star

I'm a rock star,
People believe me,
Because I am a rock star,
People say I'm good,
Because I'm a rock star,
I've been trained to be a rock star,
I'm good,
I'm cool,
I'm fantastic,
Because I am a rock star.
I can sing songs and dance
Because
I am good,
I am cool,
I am fantastic,
Because I am a rock star.

Ellie Holman   (8)
Beehive Preparatory School, Ilford

My Family

I will never find a better family
Than my own,
If I didn't have a family like I do at home,
I would be with someone else
Or on my own,
If I didn't have a family,
My friends would keep me company,
My family
Are probably the best in the world.

Arun Patel   (9)
Beehive Preparatory School, Ilford

The Playground

Our playground is fun,
It is crazy,
Everybody goes wild,
Everybody shouts,
All of the people try
And get a ball,
They always push and shove,
Most people play catch,
Most of the girls
Play with skipping ropes,
Our playground is small,
We are not allowed to run at all,
After half an hour we all go in,
I like the playground.

Rohan Warrier   (9)
Beehive Preparatory School, Ilford

My Best Secret Friend

I like my secret friend,
Because he is very kind and very good,
He also does funny jokes,
When he comes to school with me
He sits next to me,
Nobody can see him
Because he is invisible,
He sometimes helps me with my work,
But he doesn't act like a jerk,
I like my secret friend a lot.

Joshua Sokhal   (9)
Beehive Preparatory School, Ilford

My Favourite Things

I like ice cream
And cookies and bread,
Butter and cakes for tea,
Popcorn and rice and butterscotch,
Just for me,
Money and sweets,
Game Boys and Gamecubes,
Just for me,
Clothes and music,
Diamonds and rubies,
Just for me
And those are my favourite things.

Ashley Brand (8)
Beehive Preparatory School, Ilford

My Friend

I have a friend called Amy
She likes me
I like her
I've known her since we were two
We were at nursery when we met
She is seven
I am eight
We go dancing together now
But that's fun
I wish I could be in the playground with her
But we are at different schools.

Bethany Rollinson (8)
Beehive Preparatory School, Ilford

My 4 Seasons Haiku Poem

Animals are born
Flowers open wide on stems
In the morning sun

Sun is shining bright
Birds singing high in the trees
Leaves swaying gently

Leaves begin to fall
The wind is getting colder
The birds fly away

Snow's starting to fall
Branches creak in the cold wind
No one is around.

Meg Ferry (11)
Benyon Primary School, South Ockendon

Changing Seasons

Flowers blossoming
Animals are being born
Birds are singing songs

Grass is growing tall
The sun is shining brightly
In the warm blue sky

Leaves are now falling
The ground is scattered with leaves
Cold wind blows round me

Winter is now here
The sun's hidden in the clouds
Heaps of snow pile on the ground.

Tosin Bodija (10)
Benyon Primary School, South Ockendon

Seasons

Winter is dawning
The rain is falling harder
Put on your raincoats

When you go outside
Take care you do not get wet
Or you will get cold

The sun is shining
Through the dark and grey clouds
And creatures are out

Flowers a-blooming
Bees start to hunt for nectar
Lots of things have grown

Trees are standing high
But no green leaves are in sight
Now they are brown

The leaves have fallen
They have gone from brown to red
Creatures start to fast

The sun shines brightly
It's warmer than usual
It is summertime

People play outside
People play in swimming pools
People play all day.

Alex Hirst (10)
Benyon Primary School, South Ockendon

The Four Seasons Haikus

Green leaves are growing
Flowers are being watered
Wind is blowing trees

We can go and play
Lots of people are swimming
Summer is over

There are brown leaves now
Leaves are falling on the ground
Squirrels are hiding

Water is iced up
Everything is frosting up
No more leaves to see.

Jordan Bailey (11)
Benyon Primary School, South Ockendon

Shopper

I'm a stuff buyin', purse gettin',
Money spendin', bag swingin',
Staff askin', clothes lookin',
Shoe tryin', cash gettin',
Trouser fittin', tea drinkin',
Cake eatin', friend meetin',
Mate chattin', dress tryin',
Shop lookin', card gettin',
Blusher stealin', heel clickin',
Bargain huntin', cheap buyin',
Shampoo checkin', skirt shortenin',
Heel breakin', belt swingin'
Shopper!

Evie Mawby (10)
Benyon Primary School, South Ockendon

My Hips

My hips are fat,
Fat but small,
They don't suit me
Because I'm thin and tall.

If I walk past some clothes,
They will fall,
It's getting so embarrassing,
That sometimes I don't go out at all.

When I go to a food store,
I take up two chairs,
Someone wants to sit next to me,
They can't so everyone stares.

As I go home,
I stop and think,
What's making my hips look fat?
Is it pink, pink, pink?

As soon as I got home,
I put on something blue,
I realised I didn't look fat anymore,
Oh, thank you God, thank you.

Of course I wasn't going
To wear blue all the time,
Some days multicolour,
It wouldn't cost me a dime.

Bunmi Bodija (9)
Benyon Primary School, South Ockendon

Bumblebee - Haikus

Little bumblebee
Why do you mumble all day?
Little bumblebee.

Little bumblebee
Do you eat crumble for tea?
Little bumblebee.

Little bumblebee
Have you seen the sea before?
Little bumblebee.

Paris Bradley (11)
Benyon Primary School, South Ockendon

Fit Me If You Can

We are nice because we fit on your feet.
We have pointy heels so of course we are neat.
We will put you in a box if you don't wear socks.
We like to go dancing when you are wearing a dress,
But if you wear us, please look your best.
It's not a problem if you're dressed ugly,
But if you're dressed like that, don't wear me.
Polish us thrice a day but if you do, do it the normal way.

Rosie Robson (10)
Benyon Primary School, South Ockendon

Birds Haiku

Birds sing in the trees
Birds fly around in the air
The baby birds tweet.

Aaron Foy (11)
Benyon Primary School, South Ockendon

Haiku

Sea turtles swimming
The blue sea is glistening
In the golden sun.

Frankie Lloyd (10)
Benyon Primary School, South Ockendon

Haiku

Waves splash on the rocks
Dolphins jump up in the air
Sun shines on the sea.

Bekki Roberts (11)
Benyon Primary School, South Ockendon

The View Of A Dolphin

A deep diver
A high jumper

A skilful swimmer
A bow wave rider

A great glider
A fish catcher

An intelligent creature
A click talker.

Lindsey Brown (10)
Bildeston Primary School, Ipswich

A View Of A Giraffe

A giraffe
A leaf cruncher
A swift runner
A slow walker
A branch puller
An excellent listener
A spotted creature
A great animal.

Natalie Squirrell (10)
Bildeston Primary School, Ipswich

What If . . . ?

What if I were a   W hale big and blue?
What if I were a   H ippopotamus huge and hilarious?
What if I were an A dder precious and poisonous?
What if I were a   T   abby timid and tactical?

What if I were an I   nsect inky and infinite?
What if I were a   F   ox furtive and furry?

But I'm none of these, I'm me!

Alex Powell Davies (11)
Bildeston Primary School, Ipswich

Storm

Can you guess what animal I am?

R olling around in the grass,
A tiny fluffy tail,
B lack fur to camouflage in the dark,
B ouncing and leaping off furniture in the day,
I   ceberg salad is what I like,
T o my owners I'm called Storm and I'm the best.

Alice Oxford (11)
Bildeston Primary School, Ipswich

Football

Every Saturday I play footy
In sunshine, rain, sleet or snow
We score and they score
We win, they win or sometimes draw
But every week I try my best
That's all that counts
And I'm proud of that.

Liam Chinery (11)
Bildeston Primary School, Ipswich

View Of A Tiger

A wild pouncer
A sharp biter
A rapid runner
A fast striker
A flesh eater
A sly predator
An antelope killer
A tactical hunter.

James Bateson (11)
Bildeston Primary School, Ipswich

The View Of A Chicken

A grass mower
A strutty walker
A chatty talker
A dust bather
A fast runner
A hand feeder
An egg layer
A cheeky chick.

Sophie Hooper (11)
Bildeston Primary School, Ipswich

A View Of A Horse

A hurdle jumper
A graceful mover
A hay eater
A bucking bronco
A great galloper
An intelligent creature
A fast flighter
A powerful worker.

Kerie Breeze (11)
Bildeston Primary School, Ipswich

A View Of A Swan

A swift glider.
A graceful swimmer.
An angry egg layer.
A furious hisser.
An intelligent bird.
An elegant flyer.
A chick carrier.
A fierce chaser.

Sophie Brinkley (11)
Bildeston Primary School, Ipswich

Monkeys

Oh monkeys are so beautiful but also hairy
Racoons rustling through the trees
Diving in the leaves, monkeys are amazing
Eating bananas, swing from tree to tree
Running like a man, amazing to be.

Philip Shirley (10)
Bildeston Primary School, Ipswich

My Pet Tour

I have a cat her name is Keeps,
She slinks around all night,
She has sleek furry ears,
A short dark coat,
She keeps herself to herself,
That's my cat Keeps.
I have a cat, her name's Bandit,
She's fourteen years of age,
All she does is sleep and eat
And limp about the house,
Even if she's old, I love her lots,
That's my cat Bandit.
I have five chickens,
Betty, Tiger, Lion, Rosie and Issy,
They are completely dumb,
None of them have a bit of sense,
No, not even one,
All they do is scrap about,
That's all five of my chickens.
I have two fish,
All they do is swim around,
Look gormless and eat,
I have covered my house head to toe,
From the garden to the sink,
So it's time to say goodbye, the tour of my pets is over.

Charlotte Crust (10)
Bildeston Primary School, Ipswich

That's Why I Love Summer

Cricket bats, lazy cats
Men on boats with silly hats
Families on picnic mats
That's why I love summer

Lazy days and heatwaves
Fields of barley, wheat and maize
Boys and girls with fashion craze
That's why I love summer

Cold ice cream, nice to dream
Playing down by brook or stream
Fly a kite or fish for bream
That's why I love summer

Holidays far away
Large white beaches, long warm days
Wish I were somewhere nice today
I wish that it were summer.

Joel Sherwin (10)
Bildeston Primary School, Ipswich

A View Of A Horse

A swift trotter
A huge jumper
A grand winner
A fun rider
A loud runner
A graceful walker
A shiny coat
A merry neigher.

Paige Lynn (10)
Bildeston Primary School, Ipswich

Bully Rap

The oppressor, the bully,
We all know the word.
The bully in the playground,
He's just a coward.

We don't like a bully,
A bully's no good.
If you act like a bully,
You ain't in our hood.

If you pick on others,
You're being real mean.
You're a bully, no good,
You ain't in our hood.

Don't be a bully,
Get out of that trap.
Listen to our word,
It's a bully rap.

Charles Lester (10)
Bildeston Primary School, Ipswich

If I . . .

If I were an eagle I'd be flying in the sky,
If I were a mouse I'd be hiding in a field,
If I were a parrot I'd be flying through the rainforest,
If I were a deer I'd be running through a wood,
If I were a great white shark, I'd be swimming in a sea,
If I were an elephant I'd be wandering the African plains,
But I'm none of these,
I'm me.

Samuel Taylor (11)
Bildeston Primary School, Ipswich

A Mountain Poem

Fresh streams running by
Sparkling in the sun
Wild goats drinking
Pure snow untouched
The mountains' inhabitants unknown

Mountains like
Andes
Alps and
Himalayans
Tallest of the lot

All the youngest
All stand proud like kings
All princes of Earth
All as strong as iron
All greater than any man born.

Brent Walker (10)
Bildeston Primary School, Ipswich

Stars Haikus

Bring light to the sky
Glistening for all to see
The lords of the night

Darkness of midnight
Silent, nothing to be heard
The hours of black

Hours ticking by
The master of day and night
Moving too quickly.

Martin Greenacre (10)
Bildeston Primary School, Ipswich

Recipe For A Greener World

To start the spell all you have to do is . . .
Put in the stem of a sunflower,
A root of a rose,
A leaf of a lily,
Take a tablespoon of tulips,
Add a hint of holly,
A slice of tree bark,
Add a block of bushes,
Put in a bucket of bluebells,
Add the rain of a cloud,
Take the light of the sun,
A handful of hope,
Mix in with happiness and care
And now you have your spell.

Jamie Ashworth (10)
Bildeston Primary School, Ipswich

Snow

Snowflakes falling to the ground,
Touch them very carefully,
Realise how delicate they are,
Use them to make snowmen,
Cold fingers in the snow,
Throw snowballs all around,
Understand the snow will melt,
Ride on a sledge over it,
Every time, I love it.

Kitty Rodwell (10)
Bildeston Primary School, Ipswich

The Trojan War

What can you see?
Sharp, strong, shiny spears flying through the gentle air,
Strong Achilles stabbing fiercely into the backs of cowardly men,
Anxious, worried women running quickly through the
huge bronze gates,
Scared children rushing to their sobbing mothers, rushing
from the fierce men.

What can you hear?
Terrified, frightened women screaming piercingly,
Crackling, fierce, blazing fires with spitting, roaring flames
bursting brightly out,
Commanders bellowing, 'Charge!' to the fierce, strong men,
Silvery, sharp swords clashing loudly together.

What can you feel?
Heat rushing fiercely through my weak body,
My terrified mother gripping me tightly,
Red blood dripping down my sore hand,
Hatred of cold, terrifying men.

What can you taste?
The bitterness of soulless men,
Strong, airless smoke rushing past my swollen body,
Salty wet sweat dripping down my cold face,
The heat of strong, fearless fires.

What can you smell?
Flames bursting out of blazing, burning, booming fires,
The burning of weak, wet wood,
The burning of rotting bodies,
The burning of my sweet home.

Helena McColl (10)
Cherry Trees School, Bury St Edmunds

The Battle

Bows release arrows and they soar through the sky
Like bullets from a gun, firing!
Horses jump around like they're jumping on a trampoline!
As the fighting starts, a pile of fighting bodies pile up into a wall,
Anger fills the soldiers' eyes as they fight for their life.

Screams fill the dusty air like emotions bursting from bodies,
Spears and shields clash like two hundred cars banging together,
Running footsteps fill the war grounds,
Wheels from chariots crush the stone-hard ground
Like one hundred elephants standing in the same place . . .

Soldiers' heart beat so fast they might just explode
While they watch their powerful,
Vicious enemy waiting to charge at them.
They feel terrified . . .
Other soldiers hold their heads high and feel protected by the solid,
Rock-hard wall that no living thing can break!
Some soldiers scream with anger,
Acting like their body carries nothing but anger itself!
Some soldiers stare in horror when they realise
They are too injured to live any longer.
They fall to their grave and they are in bitter pain
Until their life ends with a flash as their soul
Suddenly leaves their body.

Sophie Linnett (9)
Darlinghurst Primary School, Leigh-on-Sea

The Battle

I looked all around and all I could see was dust like a thick fog,
Gradually the dust cleared away.
I could see the spears piercing people like pins popping balloons.
Down below I could see the enemy dying like wriggling worms,
I saw the horses collapsing to the floor like a wall falling to the ground.

I heard the enemies' screaming of death and the arrows whistle
Through the air like the wind howling.
The clashes of spears and shields sounded like cars
                                        crashing together.
I heard the bones of our enemies smashing like glass shattering,
I was shocked that the enemy were winning,
Like they were playing football and scoring scratches against my men.

I was proud of myself as I was still alive,
But I was frightened that I was going to get killed by
                                        my ferocious enemy,
Then suddenly I felt pain in my heart as the world went dark.

Saffron Joiner   (9)
Darlinghurst Primary School, Leigh-on-Sea

A War Poem

Aeroplanes bombing boats
People with guns ready to fire and fight
Smoke in the sky and all I feel is the heat from the bombs
My face is burning hot and bombs explode
Vast tanks move
Aeroplanes flying above me
I can hear the aeroplanes buzzing
And tanks firing their guns.

Kymberlee Webb   (9)
Darlinghurst Primary School, Leigh-on-Sea

War Poem

Men on the rocks,
A sinking boat,
An aeroplane dropping bombs
And soldiers wearing raggedy clothes.

Bony ground
And warm air,
Rocks, stones,
Wood and metal
And a bit of plastic.

The ground shaking,
Water splashing
And bombs going *boom!*
My face burning.

Michael Goose (8)
Darlinghurst Primary School, Leigh-on-Sea

The Battle

The line of spears were poised ready to pounce like a cat.
The sea of helmets clashed together,
The crimson colour of blood amongst the dull soldiers' bodies.
The horses and chariot charged menacingly
Like a rhinoceros that had just been poked.

The arrows soared through the sky like bullets from a gun.
The iceberg shields blocked their way.
Soldiers roared like lions having just been killed,
The colour of crimson flowing like water from a tap.

I felt intimidated like a harmless little spider.
In my eyes I could feel death, the scent of blood stung my nose.
At the same time I was positive we would win for our country.

Rebecca Kibria (10)
Darlinghurst Primary School, Leigh-on-Sea

The Battle

The fighting soldiers fire their deadly black arrows like
a speeding plane,
The horses carry our enemy, which make me more nervous,
I see people piled up on each other like a pile of bricks,
There is lots of blood around and people's bodies.

My army is as strong as my house,
No one could break it.

I am confident but I'm nervous
Because I see blood as red as roses.
I feel like I'm going to lose everything if I don't win,
But I know I'm going to win.
I hear people shouting as loud as thunder
And I hear pain, sickening, horrible, loud screams,
I hear the horses galloping and galloping.

Harmony Brandon (9)
Darlinghurst Primary School, Leigh-on-Sea

Troy

As I trembled with fear,
I charged forward as if a fire was spreading,
I shook holding my spear in fear,
All the tragedy . . . a metre in front of me, also inside me.
We clashed together as if we were the walls of the Red Sea.
I heard someone speaking inside of me . . .
Twang, a wave of arrows glided gracefully through the sky,
But bringing death at the end of their flight.
Piercing the skin of warriors risking their lives for their country,
War ends, silence appears,
People lie dead on the ground never to rise, to jump or pound.

Leah-May Keeble (10)
Darlinghurst Primary School, Leigh-on-Sea

The Battle

As war began, I was ordered to draw my bow and arrow to fire from,
We could see more warships coming from behind the soldiers,
All you could see from the top of the city wall was a sea of shiny silver
helmets bobbing up and down,
As soon as we shot our fire-breathing arrows it was like a tsunami of
dragons breathing their fire at the rivals.

When they got through the army wall, all I could feel were the city walls
vibrating like a nervous cannonball about to be fired at 200mph,
All I could feel was my helmet touching my delicate skin like I was
plunging my head in a boiling hot bath or sunbathing for 24 hours.

When I shoot my arrows my bow vibrates like a person
playing a guitar,
When I run out of arrows I slide down a ladder to defend my country
with a sword and I can feel scorching sand beneath my feet.

I could hear the soldiers screaming with the fright of death,
When we shot our arrows we could hear the screaming
through the city,
I could hear the soldiers piling into a wall,
I could hear the soldiers' swords clanking together like robots
having a punch-up.

Joe Arber (10) & Theo Brown (9)
Darlinghurst Primary School, Leigh-on-Sea

A War Poem

Bombs firing down,
Men getting hurt,
Boats blasting open,
My heart pounding with fear,
Boats crashing to oblivion,
Ground shaking like an earthquake.

Morgan Court (8)
Darlinghurst Primary School, Leigh-on-Sea

The Battle

The arrows like darts dashing through the sky at my charging enemy,
I'm frustrated from the sight of the enemy,
I'm more confident than the soldiers down below,
My enemy's swords shining in my eyes,
I heard my enemy clash into the soldiers down below.
I saw shining red blood all over the dusty field,
Twinkling in the light,
The weapons and soldiers were sprinkled over the dusty field.

The smashing of swords was burning my ears like fire,
I put my hands in the dust to grip my bow,
I fired my arrow, mine was different to the others,
It sounded like an eagle swooping down from above.
I'm confident like a gorilla fighting a mouse,
I'm brave like a solider but weak like an ant
Unprotected from a human's boot.

Jamie Reed (9)
Darlinghurst Primary School, Leigh-on-Sea

Troy

The people down below waiting like a hungry pride of lions,
Spears ready for war.

Fear happening so fast within us,
Like waves from the ocean crashing against the shore.

Shields charging before us,
Clashing helmets against us,
Angry people near us,
Blood on the floor.

The arrows soar through the sky
Like a sea of rage.

I am like a hungry tiger,
Waiting to kill my prey.

Jordaná Fooks (10)
Darlinghurst Primary School, Leigh-on-Sea

Battle

It was terrifying to hear the other soldiers' screams
As they piled on top of each other like a wall of bricks.
Then all of a sudden the sound of the arrows
Shooting through the air like fireworks,
The clashes of shields and spears burnt my ears
Like a bonfire going up in flames.

The horses looked like they were going to burst with anger,
As I looked, the battleground slowly turned into a crimson river
As blood poured from the bodies.
I looked around and saw all the dead lying around like sleeping lions.

Inside me I felt like I had been torn into a thousand pieces
And all my friends were amongst the dead.
I felt like I was dead myself,
I was so sad at their loss,
The ground was rough and red raw from blood.

Emily Barnes (9)
Darlinghurst Primary School, Leigh-on-Sea

Troy

From above I could see a sea of soldiers.
I saw horses trotting from side to side.
My enemy blinded me with their shields.
The arrows darted like a hurricane of death.

I heard charging horses coming at us.
I heard people shouting and crying.
The people were crashing together, it made me shiver.
I heard my side were dying by the second.

I felt like we'd lost the battle.
I felt sad and confused.
I saw scarlet-red all on the floor.
Then I heard we'd won the battle of Troy.

Kirsty Pennycook (10)
Darlinghurst Primary School, Leigh-on-Sea

The Battle

As the horses galloped, carrying weak and confused soldiers,
Others get ready to fight with baring teeth like a fierce tiger.
The shields are to protect them
And look like rabbits hopping up and down,
Then they draw their spears with horror, with anger in their voices,
The others release the arrows,
As they shoot off into the dark sky
And come down with a ping,
They come down like there is no end.

The people feel worthless and unappreciated
Of their work which endangers their lives,
On the other hand some of them are confident and feel no pain.

When the soldiers fight, other worried soldiers stare,
With astonishment in their souls,
Trying to win their battle.

Ashley Horsburgh (10)
Darlinghurst Primary School, Leigh-on-Sea

A Wartime Poem

Soldiers sliding swiftly down the muddy ground,
Crashing into massive tanks,
Air going hot and cold, hot and cold,
Each time I moved a step,
Ground shaking this way and that,
War!
Bombs blasting,
War!

Shamima Hussain (9)
Darlinghurst Primary School, Leigh-on-Sea

The Battle

The two armies met with a colossal smash
That sounded like sumo wrestlers colliding,
I could hear people screaming with a loud cry of pain,
As the enemy started to appear
The stomps got louder like a stampede!

I could feel my blood wriggling through my veins like worms,
The coldness was seeking throughout my body from my helmet,
I could feel a leathery bow and a silk bow and arrow
With slate on the end,
I can feel splitting pain off other people's hearts.

I see my men on the floor bleeding to death
Laying like an ant,
I can see the enemy's bodies laying dead too like murdered cows,
I can picture Sparta winning the battle
And then Sparta wins, *hooray!*
With 60 men left including me!

Sophie Wade (10)
Darlinghurst Primary School, Leigh-on-Sea

Troy

Blood is flowing everywhere like the tide coming in of an evening,
Horses fear the spears and shields,
The anger in their eyes tells us all,
I'm looking up at all of the arrows while they await to fire.

I hear shouting, yelling like a bull ready to charge at the enemy,
Horses gallop towards them, I hear thumping vibrations
Like volcanoes evolving.

I feel frightened, worried I might not see my family again,
When a shock, like blood rushing to my head,
Gave me confidence.

Rebecca Davis (10)
Darlinghurst Primary School, Leigh-on-Sea

The Battle

The soldiers on the other side were using the anger in their voices
To frighten us off,
Their spears were sharp like a rhinoceros' horn.
Our arrows were going so fast
They looked like a swarm of wasps,
Looking down at the helmets, it looked like the sea.

Some soldiers were screaming furiously,
The clashing of spears and shields were roaring,
The horses were stamping so hard
It sounded like an elephant,
Arrows were creating their own wind.

The spears were really heavy
Like ten bags of sugar,
They were terrified like a harmless animal,
While we were confident like a lion hunting its prey,
Some of us were in pain,
But were we going to survive?

Jack Burns (10)
Darlinghurst Primary School, Leigh-on-Sea

A World War II Senses Poem

Men dying, tanks killing,
Boats sinking, bombing other boats,
Fire in the sky,
Shooting engines from planes,
Smashing to the ground,
Me groaning,
Falling backwards as they're being shot.

Reece Farrugia (9)
Darlinghurst Primary School, Leigh-on-Sea

The Battle

The soldiers' helmets looked like black bullets waiting to be fired,
The chariots raced ahead led by horses with determination
in their eyes,
The shields are a circle of fire burning a hole in the shield
And burning the enemy's eyes.

There was so much blood,
It was like God had turned the battle area into a bloody river.
The moment the battle started I felt like I was in a maze
Because I was so frustrated, I felt like I was going to die,
The anger that was flowing through my mind,
I also felt safe because I am at the back,
Finally I heard the sound of a screaming soldier in pain
It was the sound of a newborn baby crying for its mother.

Then I heard the sound of anger,
It sounded like a building that had just been knocked over,
The shouting was very loud and clear,
The sound trembled through my ears.

Chloè Gyamfi (10)
Darlinghurst Primary School, Leigh-on-Sea

A World War II Senses Poem

Planes bombing on the land,
Bombs crashing,
Tanks on their sides,
Dead bodies laying on the ground,
Planes exploding in the air,
Smoke drifting away,
Blood dripping from bodies.

Chugging planes flying round in the sky,
Men screaming from death,
The choking engines of planes and tanks.

Gemma Andrews (8)
Darlinghurst Primary School, Leigh-on-Sea

A World War II Senses Poem

Wounded, struggling soldiers,
Climbing up clambering cliffs,
Planes all around,
Bombs on the ground,
Rusty, shattered, grey, old ships,
Scary aeroplanes dropping bombs from the sky,
Water splashing madly,
Fire blowing all around the air stupidly,
Dark, miserable ships sinking fast.

Bombs dropping, soldiers crying for more help,
Planes flying all around,
Ships crashing together,
Soldiers surrendering, ships on fire.

Pain, hot, flaming fire,
Hot, hungry, injured, lonely, tired people.

Zoe Angus (9)
Darlinghurst Primary School, Leigh-on-Sea

A World War II Senses Poem

Wounded struggling soldiers climbing up rocks,
Planes all around,
Bombs on the ground blowing up,
Rough, old, brown boats sinking fast,
Water splashing up and down,
Fire in the air like a bright sunrise.

Soldiers crying for help,
Planes dropping and making them go *bang!*
Bombed planes crashing to the ground,
Soldiers surrendering and some saying, 'Hoorah!'
Water splishing and splashing,
Bombs blowing up.

Susanna Kadur (9)
Darlinghurst Primary School, Leigh-on-Sea

A World War II Senses Poem

Black smoke as murky as a night's sky,
Planes scattering bombs around the land,
Soldiers injured struggling up the rocks,
Explosions from tanks making people scared,
Brown, tattered, dirty ships broken.

Bombs briskly falling on the ground,
Explosions bellowing down,
People screaming horrendously,
Soldiers being tormented,
Men and women's shoes running away.

Vibrations shattering by my feet,
Being scared as if monsters are attacking,
Scorching hot, as boiling as steam.

Dannielle Cohen (8)
Darlinghurst Primary School, Leigh-on-Sea

This Is The Exploding Year

Sinking ships bubbling
Bombs destroying homes and people's lives
Tanks coming in slowly
Bullets being shot by men
People screaming for help
The sound of planes speeding in
And falling in water
Water sinking into mud
Trenches muddy and disgraceful
People laying on the mud as they slowly fade away.

Jack Kerry (9)
Darlinghurst Primary School, Leigh-on-Sea

A World War II Senses Poem

War tanks exploding,
Ginormous bombs dropping suddenly from the sulky sky,
Weary soldiers clambering slowly up the rocks like wounded creatures,
Planes that are dropping bombs,
Fire about the air killing thousands,
Dead bodies lying around waiting to be dealt with,
Blood spilt all over bodies and uniforms.

Planes soaring across the sky,
People moaning and groaning searching for survival,
Exploding bombs loud enough to burst my eardrums,
My children in my mind crying out helplessly,
Trains taking poor evacuees to the country in the background,
Our sergeant commanding us to fight the enemy side,
Gunshots right behind me,
War helmets clunking together.

Zoë Newton (9)
Darlinghurst Primary School, Leigh-on-Sea

A War Poem

Men dead on the battlefield,
Torpedoes blowing up the water,
Sad, sad men losing their lives.

Stones flying through the air,
My children crying for my love in my soul,
My heart beating for life.

Men shouting for my help,
Bombs exploding,
Screaming in every ear.

William Medhurst (8)
Darlinghurst Primary School, Leigh-on-Sea

A World War II Senses Poem

Planes bombing big black boats,
Nose-diving into the sea,
Men clambering up the big mountain rocks like ants,
Tanks driving quickly out of massive blue boats,
Flames blazing out of the sea,
Boats sinking into the dark water,
Like an island sinking.

Planes' bombs going off,
Soldiers dying in the background,
Soldiers screaming in fright.

Worried about my relatives,
Scared about if I was going to die or not,
I felt scared because of the destruction.

Andrew Livett (9)
Darlinghurst Primary School, Leigh-on-Sea

A War Poem

Bombs exploding
Vast tanks rolling slowly like snails
Leaving track marks
Bombs exploding again and again

Hot, burning bombs
Chunks of flying stone in the air
I can feel bits of rubber from the tanks
Holes in the ground

Tanks rumbling across the grass
Bombs are exploding
People crying for their lives
Troops running across the grass
And rumbling the ground.

Cy Daly (8)
Darlinghurst Primary School, Leigh-on-Sea

A War Poem

Men holding guns and shooting in the air
Planes rumbling across the sky
Bombs dropping like marbles
Boats bobbing in the water
Rocked by waves
And heading this way
And boats exploding!
Smoke everywhere.

Tara King (9)
Darlinghurst Primary School, Leigh-on-Sea

A World War II Senses Poem

Brave soldiers risking their lives,
Explosions as aeroplanes fall from the grey smoky sky,
Ships sinking one by one into the deep blue sea,
Badly injured men laying on the dusty beach,
Men being pushed off mountains and killed with large guns,
Men scurrying to land before their red ships get bombed,
Waves as rough as the garden hose on full blast.

Helen Archer (8)
Darlinghurst Primary School, Leigh-on-Sea

A Wartime Poem

Bombs exploding,
Ships sinking,
Blasting bombs,
Dropping like marbles,
Feel the sadness,
Feel the fear.

Jade Hall (8)
Darlinghurst Primary School, Leigh-on-Sea

A World War II Senses Poem

Smashed planes,
Bombs and fire,
Smoke in the air,
Where bombs have exploded,
Camouflaged tanks.

The sea looks like millions of bombs
Have been bashed and crashed near the shore,
It is like the sea is on fire.

Robyn Walton (8)
Darlinghurst Primary School, Leigh-on-Sea

A World War II Senses Poem

Men dying like flies
And bombs being dropped,
It all seemed like a dream
And there I was standing in the middle of the terrifying war.

I could hear the screaming soldiers,
Bombs exploding,
Planes smashing to the ground.

Aidan Romero Muñoz (8)
Darlinghurst Primary School, Leigh-on-Sea

Troy

We are racing like rhinos as we charged.
Our bright shiny armour reflected from the sun.
I was given my orders, fire then *twang!*
They let the arrows glance like a wave of death.
As the enemy approached, my heart ached with terror.

Gauge Salter (9)
Darlinghurst Primary School, Leigh-on-Sea

This Is The Horrible Year!

Vast tanks surrounding people,
Leaving tracks like a snail,
Tanks shooting soldiers while popping in and out of the trenches,
Blasting bombs dropping like marbles,
Bombs burning my face,
Mud sticking to me,
Blood rushing round me like the mud in the air,
Engines deafening people and me.

Shannon Willson (9)
Darlinghurst Primary School, Leigh-on-Sea

A War Poem

Boats being bombed at the end of the harbour,
Men fighting for their lives,
Exploding bombs flying everywhere,
Violence coming down on us,
Hot smoke in my eyes,
Lumps of wood still burning,
Hot coal burning my feet,
Bombs dropping densely, almost crashing.

Ella Dakin (8)
Darlinghurst Primary School, Leigh-on-Sea

A War Poem

Blasting bombs dropping densely like marbles,
Tanks shaking the floor
And they were shaking the floor like a toy hitting the ground.

George Haley (9)
Darlinghurst Primary School, Leigh-on-Sea

Troy

I can see . . .

Soldiers moving like ants, their armour as a new penny,
Horses as brown as glossy mud, waiting to go to war.
The ground is as dusty as a desert and as dry as my mouth.
I can see my life flashing beyond my eyes.

I can hear . . .

Arrows pinging like shooting stars as soldiers roared like lions,
Armour rattling as the horses thunder along.

I can touch . . .

I can feel the sharp spear being pushed through my chest
                                                        like cold ice,
As the enemy approached my heavy archers fire with arrows.

Billy Blewitt (10)
Darlinghurst Primary School, Leigh-on-Sea

Tsunami

A beach-wrecker
A heart-breaker
A family-splitter
A world-changer
A life-ruiner
A sea-mover
A natural-disaster
A home-shaker

We think of those in pain.

Danielle Barwick (10)
Godwin Primary School, Dagenham

Ode To A Jacket

O snugly jacket,
How you keep me looking good on a cold winter's day,
It's like a fashion show,
I love the way you sparkle when you're resting on the hook.
When I pick you up you are ready to show off.
You make me look like a million dollars,
Like you're unaffordable.
O lovely jacket of mine!

Abigail Parker (10)
Godwin Primary School, Dagenham

The Tsunami

A fear-bringer,
A life-ruiner,
A family-breaker,
A home-destroyer,
A world-splitter,
A natural-disaster.

Why do these things happen?

Hannah Stanley (10)
Godwin Primary School, Dagenham

A Rainy Day

A puddle-maker,
An umbrella-splasher,
A plant-waterer,
A people-wetter,
A flood-starter,
An ice-maker,
A rainy day.

Sara Rayment (10)
Godwin Primary School, Dagenham

Tsunami

A beach-blower,
A sea-shaker,
A house-wrecker,
A family-breaker,
A moving-disaster,
The tsunami.

Victoria Heed (10)
Godwin Primary School, Dagenham

Feelings

Happiness is as blue as the great deep ocean's horizon,
Happiness tastes like curry, in the most hottest desert,
Happiness looks like Heaven, so very, very calm and peaceful,
Happiness sounds like Busted, at the biggest crowd of
                                    people in the world,
Happiness feels like a sponge ball, squishing in my hand
                                    as I go to kick it.

Connor Jackson (10)
Gunthorpe Primary School, Peterborough

Feelings

Happiness is white, as a light cloud and a pretty daisy,
Happiness smells like a breath of passion in the air,
Happiness looks like a massive big ball, full of shiny crystals,
Happiness feels like chocolate, dripping and melting from
                                    the bright and colourful sun,
Happiness tastes like warm dessert custard.

Emma Sansom (9)
Gunthorpe Primary School, Peterborough

Feelings

Happiness is yellow, as yellow as the
beautiful golden yellow sun.

Happiness tastes like a lovely cake,
with yellow icing dropping down the cake.

Happiness smells like six hot dogs
burning on the golden beach.

Happiness looks like the golden sun
settling down.

Happiness sounds like the waves
crashing against the huge rocks.

Happiness feels like a lovely
princess dancing in the sunset.

Lauren Maloney (10)
Gunthorpe Primary School, Peterborough

Feelings

Happiness is yellow, as yellow as bright golden sand.
Happiness smells like water when I'm swimming beneath the ocean.
Happiness tastes like Coke skating down my throat.
Happiness sounds like raindrops falling from the dark, cloudy sky.
Happiness feels like the shiny skin of a whale jumping over the wave.

Sophie Emery (9)
Gunthorpe Primary School, Peterborough

Calmness

Calmness is silver, as the silver wind blowing the trees.
Calmness tastes like hot chocolate swirling round my mouth.
Calmness smells like calm wind drifting in the cool air.

Jack Dolby (9)
Gunthorpe Primary School, Peterborough

Feelings

Happiness is as yellow as the beautiful yellow sun.
Happiness tastes like candyfloss bubbling in my mouth.
Happiness smells like a red-hot burning flame.
Happiness looks like Busted when I went to see them.
Happiness sounds like my favourite Busted CD.
Happiness feels like me munching a big bag of sweets.

Georgia Calver (9)
Gunthorpe Primary School, Peterborough

Feelings

Happiness is yellow, as the bright sun in the sky.
Happiness tastes like chocolate dripping down my gullet.
Happiness smells like freshness, breeze in the air.
Happiness looks like the bright blue sea, rushing against the rocks.
Happiness sounds like FM radio playing in my head.
Happiness feels like you want to surf on the blue sea.

Ranasha Lotmore (9)
Gunthorpe Primary School, Peterborough

Feelings

Happiness is pink, as pink as a lovely pink rose,
Happiness tastes like candyfloss sticking to my nose at the fair.
Happiness smells like hot dogs on the hot dog stand sizzling in a pan.
Happiness looks like a flower drifting from side to side in the breeze.
Happiness sounds like me and my friends having fun in the park.
Happiness feels like a dancer, dancing on the golden sand.

Emma Holman (9)
Gunthorpe Primary School, Peterborough

Happiness

Happiness is gold, gold as the golden star.
Happiness tastes like chocolate, deliciously melting down my throat.
Happiness smells like a barbecue sizzling.
Happiness sounds like dreamy music, dreamily sounding
                                    out of the speakers.
Happiness sounds like a lovely book being read in the sun.
Happiness feels like a hug, keeping you as warm as the sun.

Karina Mayes (9)
Gunthorpe Primary School, Peterborough

Happiness

Happiness is like the yellow, hot, boiling sun in the bright blue sky.
Happiness smells like a roast dinner baking in the hot oven.
Happiness looks like the sunset rising ready for the dawn.
Happiness sounds like the gentle sea coming into shore.
Happiness feels like I am having a wonderful party with disco lights.
Happiness tastes like candyfloss melting in my mouth.

Shona Warren (9)
Gunthorpe Primary School, Peterborough

Happiness

Happiness is orange as the bulging sun in our solar system.
Happiness smells like a baking doughnut in the baker's shop.
Happiness tastes like a fresh strawberry.
Happiness looks like a beautiful rainbow over the blue sky.
Happiness sounds like a ferry's horn in the grey mist.
Happiness feels like you're floating on funny-shaped white clouds.

Joel Grenfell (10)
Gunthorpe Primary School, Peterborough

Happiness

Happiness is gold, gold in a cave
waiting to be found.

Happiness tastes like roast dinner on the table
waiting to go down my throat.

Happiness looks like a golden sun
shimmering in the sky.

Happiness sounds like children
playing on the beach.

Happiness feels like ice cream
slowly drifting down my throat.

Paige Cann (9)
Gunthorpe Primary School, Peterborough

Happiness

Happiness is red, as a rose sitting on a rosebush.
Happiness tastes like grilled bacon on a BBQ.
Happiness smells like a sweet strawberry on the table.
Happiness looks like white creamy sensation chocolate in a box.
Happiness sounds like calm music in a church.
Happiness feels like a soft teddy cuddling me tight.

Chelsey Etherington (9)
Gunthorpe Primary School, Peterborough

Feelings

Happiness is yellow, as yellow as the bright sun.
Happiness tastes like chocolate in my mouth.
Happiness smells like ice cream far away in a cornet.
Happiness looks like cats playing with colourful string.
Happiness sounds like calm CDs.
Happiness feels like sand running down your hands.

Amy Clipston (9)
Gunthorpe Primary School, Peterborough

Feelings

Happiness is purple, as purple as a gigantic violet
sitting on a violet bush.

Happiness tastes like a huge cookie,
crunching in my mouth.

Happiness smells like a big juicy hot dog
sizzling in the oven.

Happiness looks like a big ice cream
melting in my hand.

Happiness sounds like a bumblebee
buzzing in my ear.

Happiness feels like a lovely holiday abroad
on a desert island.

Adam Lomas (10)
Gunthorpe Primary School, Peterborough

The Moon

The moon turning very slowly,
As the people run like mad.
The moon as mysterious as can be,
The moon turning very slowly.

The moon turning very slowly,
As white as can be.
The moon damp and cold,
The moon turning very slowly.

The moon turning very slowly,
Moon, moon come down.
Moon, moon come up,
The moon turning very slowly.

Nicola Anderson (9)
Gunthorpe Primary School, Peterborough

Feelings

Happiness is orange, as orange as a bright light
shimmering down on me.

Happiness tastes like chocolate melting in my mouth,
dripping down my throat.

Happiness smells like a lovely red rose
in the swaying calm wind.

Happiness looks like a beautiful portrait
hanging on the wall.

Happiness sounds like a lovely quiet piece
of Indian music.

Happiness feels like a nice, hot, bubbly bath.

Scott Sherriff (9)
Gunthorpe Primary School, Peterborough

Feelings

Happiness is as white as the white freezing snow,
melting as the sun comes up in the brand new morning.

Happiness tastes like hot chocolate rushing down my throat
the same way as a train.

Happiness smells like hot burning sausages on a barbecue
as they go *sizzle, pop, bang.*

Happiness looks like a scene of a beach
with waves running along the surface of the sea.

Happiness sounds like people playing and talking happily.

Happiness feels like a soft teddy, cuddling me really gently.

Jade Lowbridge (9)
Gunthorpe Primary School, Peterborough

The Hill Of Death

In the sunrisen bay, murderous Persians huddle and plan their war.
Deaf to the danger that is hidden in the hills.
The Athenians, powerful and patient, slink like cats stalking their prey.

Athenians charge at the unsuspecting Persians,
Like a mouse, shooting through a hungry cat's legs.
The sea beats against the now blood-red sand as swords clunk.
The sound of death which many ears hear,
Tomato-red blood oozing from heads,
Helpless dead bodies hitting the sand that has been turned scarlet.
Men's shrieks penetrate the once silent air
As they try, in the few seconds left, to grasp,
They are dying,
26 miles for a weak runner to run.

Bolting to tell the great news,
The Athenians had won,
Exhaustion carried the sprinter into a deep sleep
From which no one could wake him.

Rachael Bartlett (10)
Holy Trinity CE Primary School, Colchester

The Greek War

In the isolated bay, the Persians prepare for their awaited battle.
Quiet and calm, yet under the surface they are sick with
nerves and fear.
Determined to win, the devious Athenians observe their targets
with the keenness of an eagle.

Slinking forward, the Athenians advance,
Scrutinising the Persians, their eyes never leaving them.
Soon, the stench of battle was in the air.
Pools of blood and the screams of scared, dying men
Piercing through the air, like a dart heading for the bullseye.
The sweet summer breeze now tainted with the smell of rotting flesh.

Silence. The boats of the Persians were full and were sailing back
towards the peaceful territory they called home.
Cheers rose up through the victorious Athenians.
The victory messenger was on his way, dashing the 26 miles.
Exhaustion flooded through him, the news was told and
he slept forever.

Charlotte Peck (11)
Holy Trinity CE Primary School, Colchester

The War

Clever and menacing the Athenians are,
Waiting patiently and well prepared to attack the unprepared Persians.
Pounding powerfully Athenians rose over the hill,
Determined and confident.
They looked scary but the Persians didn't do anything.

As the Athenians were getting closer, the Persians looked surprised,
Frightened, it looks like the Persians are going to crumble.
Athenians are hurtling down the hill,
Persians astonished, Athenians urging on in anger.
Advancing on through the misty morning sunlight,
Swords clashing and armour bashing, people dying, people crying.

The Persian army are frightened, they go away, heading
                                        towards the boats,
Athenians come off better, with scarlet-red blood dripping from the
bodies of the people who have suffered.
A runner, an Athenian messenger, ran back to Marathon as he
                                reached there he was exhausted.

Jack Gatland (10)
Holy Trinity CE Primary School, Colchester

Greek War

Brooding Persians huddled together
Under a towering block of hill.
Preparing for the fight awaiting them,
The Athenians as cunning as a leopard stalking its prey.

The leopard pounces, finally smelling
The disorganised Persians,
But they are too quick,
Blood oozes out of the poor attackers' heads,
Destroying the lives of most innocent people.
Thick, deep, crimson blood flows over the rocky floor
Like the Red Sea, a lake of hatred and betrayal.

Dead bodies lie over the cold ground,
Blood flowing on exhausted souls,
The battle has been won over,
A messenger ran the race of 26 miles,
Hurtling from Athens all the way to Marathon.
He delivered the message, fell
And entered another world.

Holly Garwood (10)
Holy Trinity CE Primary School, Colchester

Athenians' Victory

Cunning Athenians creeping up the sloping hill,
Like a lion stalking its prey,
Scorching sun burning their backs,
Pathetic Persians gloating below,
Not ready for attack.

At last, Athenians pounced on the surprised Persians,
A battle arose in the warm air of marathon.
The Athenians are a raging bull charging.
Persian after Persian dropped down dead,
Blood gushing out of bodies,
Scarlet and wet,
Dripping on the floor.
Shrieks filled the air,
As swords and spears hit the ground.

After hours of fierce fighting,
The Persians finally gave in,
King Darias furious at the clever, cunning Athenians,
A messenger was sent to share the news,
But collapsed in a heap from exhaustion and died.

Isobel Scott (10)
Holy Trinity CE Primary School, Colchester

Going To War With Persia

Athenians, menacing Athenians, ready to pounce at any moment,
A cat chasing a mouse.
Persians, unsuspecting Persians, preparing for battle
With Athens, but not quite ready.
Sneaking swiftly to the peak of the Marathon hill,
Circulating the Persians they prepare to invade.
Stealing to the top, Athenians strike.
Charging to victory, they attack.
Swords clashing, shields bashing, arrows are jet planes,
Zooming around mercilessly, their only aim to kill.
Dead bodies were in their thousands and blood-curdling shrieks
Pierced the air.
Persia's leader Darius retreats, the army pursue,
Like a lion after an antelope.
Athens' victorious leader sends a message with a slave.
The slave ran like a spine-tailed swift
But mercilessly died like a run-down battery
Delivering the message,
But it was victory!

Emily Balls (9)
Holy Trinity CE Primary School, Colchester

The Battle

Unaware powerful Persians, perched on rocks,
Sharpening blades and daggers,
A glowing sun burning, as though the people
Are trapped inside an oven.
Upon the hill, Athenians watch, waiting to pounce like predators.
In the distance, waves crashing against the sharp, cracked cliffs.
Waiting, waiting for the unpredictable future . . .

Athenians have progressed, swiftly forwards like a sailing boat
In the Pacific Ocean.
'Fight!' the leader roared, his spear in the air as sharp
And pointed as an owl's talon.
Scarlet-red blood oozing rapidly, deep bellows of pain,
Clanging of armour, a hard battle with uneven teams.

Persians escape on the racing warships off back to their homeland.
Athenians leap with joy because of victory.
Rotting bodies scattered over the stained ground.
A solitary messenger sent back to tell the news of a battle well fought.
Twenty-six miles he ran from Marathon,
Exhausted, injured, he slipped to an everlasting sleep.

Holly Morgan (10)
Holy Trinity CE Primary School, Colchester

The War

Persians unaware of Athenians,
Preparing steadily for battle.
Sword, shield, spears in shaking Persian hands
As Athenians crave for prey.
Powerful weapons built for battle ready on the olive hill.
Athenians determined to kill with crafty,
Cunning plots like owls hunting viciously for mice.

Athenians worming their way towards Persians,
Clattering armour as they sprinted at the unprepared Persians,
Fighting everywhere with spitting crimson-red blood
Like an elephant spraying water.
Shrieks, screams, shouts from every corner, nowhere is safe.
Lying on the floor ruby-red blood gushing out like red paint being spilt.
Falling to the floor like a sack of potatoes.
Quick, sudden death.

The Persians dashed to boats without stopping.
Athenians meet victory with a cheer, a messenger on the way.
Messenger manages to sprint 26 miles to tell news to Athens,
Without a noise, he falls peacefully to the floor into a deep sleep.

Samantha Payne (11)
Holy Trinity CE Primary School, Colchester

A Battle Won By Skill

Athens' army assemble around the hilly landscape
Like a gang going to exploit their enemy,
The Persians calculate their bloodshed plan
Like a magpie planning its thievery.

As the Persians work out their war,
The Athenians grow impatient
Like a roaring chariot waiting for the horse to be forced forward,
So the battle clashed like a sword fight
Being fought by two menacing sides over something so simple.
The seaweed-green grass turned to a graveyard
With screams and yells all over the battlefield.

As the Persian death toll rose
King Darius got slightly worried
Even though he started with twenty thousand men,
As he commanded the soldiers to go to the boats,
His angry head was devising an attack plan,
But that was soon wiped out by the amount
Of weapons being thrown by the Athenians.
After the battle, a messenger was sent from Athens to Persia
To tell of the Athenians' victory over a country 26 miles away,
The vicious battle was over!

James Bowles (10)
Holy Trinity CE Primary School, Colchester

The Battle

Athenians rise from the hill
Rises from the new day.

They huddle on the hillside
Prepared to fight fiercely.

Athenians shout, 'We want war!'
Athenians looked at the angry Persians,
Athenians charge!

Athenians charge into war,
They see spears, daggers, swords
Fly in the battle.

Leaders say, 'Charge'
And the battle begins.
Lots of the army were killed
And all that was left was blood,
Families were devastated.
Tears of pain came down the breathless body,
Persians race to the boats
And escape from the Athenians.

One sole messenger had to run 26 miles,
Then died.

Carl Hollingshead (10)
Holy Trinity CE Primary School, Colchester

The Doors Of War

Stalking their ant-like prey the courageous Athenians spy
Like an eagle onto a mouse.
The fiery sun burns on their backs
As they rise like a swan from the water.
Daring Athenians race towards an army opening the doors of war.

Hearing the sounds of death and pain
The war takes place on a bloody day.
The Athenians fought with one thing in their hearts,
To win that dreadful war.
Blood drips like a tap with the only difference
The water is scarlet-red and has a life hidden away inside it.
You can taste the burnt sorrow of death,
Death and pain all over the land.
Angry the Athenians, their arms like branches from an ancient tree,
Life is being taken away like candy from a baby.

Fourteen-thousand Persians run to their boats
Like wildebeest from a cheetah.
With pain and sorrow in their hearts
They know not to fight again.
A messenger tears to Athens to tell the amazing news.
Joy spread around and spirits lifted
'Cause they found they had won a terrible war.
Speaking last word bringing joy to people in Athens.

Hazel King (10)
Holy Trinity CE Primary School, Colchester

The Battle Begins

Intelligent, ingenious Athenians waiting to stalk their prey - Persians.
As the Athenians advance up from the hill,
Persians no clue of what was going on,
To notice the plan and thought of a clever, cunning Athenian,
Too busy preparing to notice.

Athenians rage to the Persians,
Up from the calm hill, charging like a bull.
Booming, shouting, the Athenians and Persians battle.
Deafening and noisy it was, like a thousand elephants zooming past.

Persians followed through the scarlet-red blood
As their leader ordered them to do so.
Sorrowful were the Persians,
Victorious Athenians sent a messenger back home.
26 long miles, exhausting it was as he fell down so tired,
It was time for him to go, for him to rest in peace.

Rebecca Herbert (10)
Holy Trinity CE Primary School, Colchester

Army Against Army

Powerful, patient Athenians,
Quietly crept up to the hill.
Athenians roared down the hill
Like a rampaging herd of elephants.
King Darius was astounded at their clever, cunning plan.
Dangerous, determined Persians were unprepared to fight.
Army against army, fought a terrible tough fight.
Thousands fought, thousands died.
Ruby-red blood trickled out of so many bodies.
The dead bodies sent off a smelly stench.
A frightened King Darius ordered the Persians to get to the boats.
A tough, tired messenger was sent to Marathon.
He told the terrific news that Athenians had won.

Rachael Weighill (10)
Holy Trinity CE Primary School, Colchester

The Clever Athenians

Hardworking Persians preparing for battle,
Not knowing that the ingenious, intelligent Athenians
are waiting patiently,
Being deafened by the booming sound of Persians hurrying,
Brave and strong the Athenians determined in their plan.

Callinachus, commander of the Athenians
Decided to charge into battle . . .
Persians confused why Athenians are rushing towards them,
All of them leap for their swords, grab their spears and charge.
Scarlet-red blood squirting from their wounds.
Violence everywhere, you could not get away.
Losing, the Persians retreated.
Escaped to their ships and sailed away.
Athenians sent a messenger to Marathon to tell the news,
Sprinting 26 miles exhausted,
Just managing to tell the news before shipping into his next life.

Jordan Lateward (11)
Holy Trinity CE Primary School, Colchester

The Battle

The Athenian army rushes towards the Persians,
Like a cheetah stalking its prey,
Powerful Persians waited patiently ready to fight.

Charging towards them they sliced out their swords
And raged towards their tummies.
As the swords went in, scarlet-red blood oozed out.

What was left of the Persians escaped,
Running to the boat sorrowfully.
As the victory runner ran 26 miles and finally got there,
Rabbiting the news.
He collapsed, running out of oxygen,
The end for him.

Annabelle Matthews (10)
Holy Trinity CE Primary School, Colchester

The War

The sea was silent, motionless, after spitting out the
                                    Persians onto land.
Angry Persians prepare for battle, not knowing they are
                                    being watched.
Cunning Athenians sit, patiently hunting their prey.

Creeping up the hill the Athenians closed in on the Persians,
                                    like an overflowing sink,
Suddenly a roar, like thunder but louder,
Angry Athenians raced towards surprised Persians,
A spear thrown, a rush towards weapons, a scream,
A scream so piercing it could deafen you,
The unprepared battle begins,
A clash of thunder, like an angry gorilla
Jumping furiously in his cage,
All different shades of blood squirting from people,
A scream,
A yell for help,
All around the smell of fresh meat,
Blood, different shades, ruby, garnet, scarlet, every shade
                                    of red under the sun.

Silence,
The battle had ended,
Athenians won,
Persians escaped by sea,
Athenians cheered,
A solitary runner raced to Athens from Marathon.
He ran 26 miles,
He told the news,
These were his last ever words,
There he fell to the ground,
He lay there motionless like all those in the battlefield.

Hayley Kelsey (11)
Holy Trinity CE Primary School, Colchester

The Battle Commences

Athenians marching up to the top of the hill,
Roasting in the sun and well prepared for battle,
Meanwhile Persians thought they were well prepared
But they weren't.

Athenians advancing to battle, raging towards the enemy,
The battle commences,
All you could see was red-ruby blood and guts
Gushing out, spears and swords dispersed,
The Persians sprinted to their boats, they escaped,
Victory for the Athenians.

A messenger is sent to Athens, 26 miles away,
He was on his way as he got there to spread the word,
After all that he was so out of breath
He crashed to the ground.

Kyle Smith (10)
Holy Trinity CE Primary School, Colchester

The Battle Between Athens And Persia

Determined, strong Athenians glaring down on the Persians
                                    looking like ants.
Like a waterfall rushing down to drown the creepy Persians.

The battle's nearly on, they can now smell the mean sense
                              of the fight about to start.
They flinch with pain as they pulled their swords out of their pouches,
Swords bashing, blood gushing like a stormy day about to begin.

14 thousand Persians rushed towards a boat,
All squashed in so the fight could be over.
Racing with good news, he dashes 26 miles to tell everyone,
But then there was a crash.
There he was lying on the floor, not breathing,
Just silent forever.

Gemma Dove (11)
Holy Trinity CE Primary School, Colchester

The Battle Of Persia

Powerful, patient Athenians lingering in the hilltops
Watching over their destiny like a lion hunting prey.
Gazing down on the Persian army noticing the weak points.
Athenians clutching swords they made, thinking about the
                                        battle that is commencing.

Appearing on the hilltop like termites on their mound.
Charging at the Persian army like geese migrating to Canada.
Menacing shouts of horror as Persians draw their swords.
Clattering crashing of archers' arrows and people dropping dead.
Spilt blood can be smelt, lives lost.
Scarlet-red blood oozes from the thousands dead.
Persians taken by surprise spear their enemy as they die.

Persians flee as they fear they may be beaten,
They flee to their boats as the Athenians chase them like a hungry cat.
Athenians embrace as victory can be smelt from blood that was spilt.
Solitary runner to tell victory is true.

Alex Cronin (11)
Holy Trinity CE Primary School, Colchester

Stormy Seas

I'm the tall ship just leaving port,
It is so windy and stormy, I wish the captain would abort.

To sail the big wide ocean we must,
Me, the crew and the captain we trust.

Day and night we ride the waves,
The nights are so dark they are like deep caves.

My sail's so full, it's going to split,
A man in the crow's nest is looking for rocks that I pray we won't hit.

The storm's nearly over, the journey nearing an end.
The port is in view, so to the seabed my anchor I'll send.

Becky Davies (11)
Holy Trinity CE Primary School, Colchester

The Siege Of Greek War

Persian soldiers organising their army
Unaware of the Athenians stalking them.
While the outrun was large
The Athenians were not to be beaten.
For they were small in size but rich with ideas,
Cunning Athenians hidden away by a hill hiding them from view.

Prepared Athenians dashing down a hill,
Shocked Persians dashing at Athenians, hearts drumming,
Battle seizing the air, swords lashing out,
Swords are drawn in, bloodied thick and red,
Athenians, overpowering the falling Persians,
Persians, helpless in a world of blood.

Stranded Persians cut off from escape,
Glimmer of hope has to be grasped,
Persians retreat as quick as a flash,
A messenger sprints away to tell of Athens victory,
The news he tells are his last words.

Katie O'Brien (10)
Holy Trinity CE Primary School, Colchester

Playgrounds

P laygrounds are big and we have lots of fun,
L aughing and playing with everyone,
A ll of the teachers are there to look out,
Y ou can ask them for help, if you don't shout!
G irls and boys, we all play the same,
'R un outs' and 'Had' and all sorts of games.
O ut in the sunshine but never the rain,
U ndercover we go to drive teachers insane!
N aughty children get put in the hall, for
D oing something bad like kicking a ball.
S o tomorrow again we look forward to play,
    Between our lessons of another day!

Brooke Saunders (9)
Lee Chapel Primary School, Basildon

My Magic Box Poem

(Based on 'Magic Box' by Kit Wright)

I will put in my box . . .
The smell of sizzling bacon
The shining Northern Lights
And the sparkling sounds of fire
Ancient Rome
Glittering fireworks and
The mountains of the Himalayas
Jolly happiness
Lovely laughter
And a nice warm bath
Some silly creatures
A giant battleship
And my own base

My box is made of . . .
Wood and steel and other elements

In my box I can turn into a dragon
And walk up to Heaven.

Tom Harvey (8)
Mayfield Primary School, Cambridge

The Blackout

Blackout!
Watch out for the cars.
Blackout!
Don't trip or fall.
Blackout!
Listen out for the siren.
Blackout!
The bikes could run you over.
Blackout!
Build a bomb shelter.
Blackout!

Joseph Harvey (8)
Mayfield Primary School, Cambridge

The Blitz

The city is black, the city is dark
The enemy bombers are near
I ran to a shelter, not failing to hear
The enemy bombers are near
The shelter collapses just as I'm near
The enemy bombers are here!
I trip over a dustbin and fall flat on the ground,
I get up again without making a sound,
The enemy bombers are here!
I trip over dustbins, I fell over cans,
The enemy bombers are here!
The people are running and fading away,
The enemy bombers are here!
I'm dashing about with an ache in my head,
The enemy bombers are here!
The sirens are blasting, the people are screaming,
The moment of death is here!

Benjamin Winger (9)
Mayfield Primary School, Cambridge

My Brilliant Friend, Marta

(Based on 'My Brilliant Friend' by Roger McGough)

She's brilliant at writing
She's brilliant at drawing
She's brilliant at reading
But sometimes it's boring

She's brilliant at music
She's brilliant at art
She's brilliant at drama
Remembering a part

She's brilliant at geography
She's brilliant at literacy
She's brilliant at playing
It's good when she plays with me!

Oliver Dawes (9)
Mayfield Primary School, Cambridge

Pollution Solution

Beware
Beware
Beware
They will creep
They will jump
You will shout
You will scream
It's the Elemonk, the Scorpispider and the Fizzwonk
You leave pollution
And don't care to make a solution
They know that they will soon be extinct
They know that soon or later they will be gone in the dirty air
So
Beware
Beware
Beware
And make a solution to try and stop
Pollution!

Phoebe Bostock (8)
Mayfield Primary School, Cambridge

Football

My friend likes football so do I,
My friend scores, so I score,
My friend passes, I pass back,
My friend is a good team player
Because she works with me!
We always meet at the park,
We play against my dad,
We always win
Because we are a *team!*

Sophie Tullett (8)
Mayfield Primary School, Cambridge

Magic Box Poem
(Based on 'Magic Box' by Kit Wright)

I will put in my box . . .
The sound of the sea swishing,
The smell of white roses
And the sound of the wind blowing.

I will put in my box . . .
The place where we watch movies
The place where we go fishing
And the place where we go hunting.

I will put in my box . . .
The kings of every country,
The President of the United States
And the most powerful person in the world.

I will put in my box . . .
The heart of the dragon
The feathers of an eagle
The tails of rats
And the feet of Martians.

My box is made of . . .
Blue whale skin
Feathers of an eagle
And tail of rats.

In my box I will go to . . .
The beach
And then go to Switzerland.

Soo-Suk Lee   (8)
Mayfield Primary School, Cambridge

My Magic Box

(Based on 'Magic Box' by Kit Wright)

I will put in my magic box . . .
the sound of the silver seashore
the smell of juicy orange oranges
and the sound of a newborn baby's cry

I will put in my magic box . . .
the orange sight of the orange sunset
the sight of multicoloured fireworks
and the tropical Hawaiian beach

I will put in my magic box . . .
the feeling of the silky sand under my feet
the feeling of the red-hot burning sun upon my skin
and the feeling of the cold air swishing through my hair

I will put in my magic box . . .
a Santa with curled pointed ears
an elf with a big cloudy beard
and an imaginary friend

My magic box is made of . . .
magic glitter
soft fur from a soft cloud
and dinosaurs' nails to close it like a locket
and a magic spell!

In my magic box I will . . .
swim with singing dolphins and whales
I will visit the octopuses in the Atlantic Ocean.

Mara Pintilie (9)
Mayfield Primary School, Cambridge

Magic Box Poem

(Based on 'Magic Box' by Kit Wright)

I will put in my box . . .
The sound of waves crashing
The sound of the clock ticking
The smell of red roses

I will put in my box . . .
The place where we buy food
The place where we catch fish
And the place where we play games

I will put in my box . . .
People with sad feelings
The Queen of England
The weakest person in the world

I will put in my box . . .
The eye of aliens
An angel on a plane
And a fish warrior

My box is made of . . .
Blue sapphires, red rubies, green emeralds

In my box I will . . .
Go to the beach
And then go bowling.

Alex Cosme (8)
Mayfield Primary School, Cambridge

Magic Box

(Based on 'Magic Box' by Kit Wright)

I will put in my box . . .
Fresh fishy smell of the sea
Delicious strawberry ice cream smells

I will put in my box . . .
Giant, wonderful Eiffel Tower scene
Funny and interesting Jeremy James books
Comfortable big red chairs

I will put in my box . . .
Stars which make us a beautiful bright sky
A cute baby crying like a bright red sunset
An angry baby crying like a nasty witch

I will put in my box . . .
A clever dictionary with a robot
And a brand new bear
Lots of presents from fat Santa Claus

My box is made with a big golden star in each corner
And it is covered with sparkles
Wood and 100 small golden silver crystals

In my box I will . . .
Put in Disney Land with kind Disney
And dance with a famous pop star.

Connie Kim (9)
Mayfield Primary School, Cambridge

My Magic Box

(Based on 'Magic Box' by Kit Wright)

I will put in my box . . .
The smell of skill,
My father's warm, rumbling voice,
The sound of a seagull swimming.

I will put in my box . . .
The cold crimson sea beneath the watery sunset,
I would like to live in one of these Christmas scenes.

I will put in my box . . .
The soft velvety feeling of creamy cushions
And the misty make-up of my mum,
Some sweet, spicy peppers.

I will put in my box . . .
A powerful, perfumed princess,
A daring, dangerous dragon
And four little aliens shopping.

My box is made of . . .
Golden dreams with eleven ruby hinges
And silver ice stands on the inside
Is the feeling of icy scales.

In my box I will . . .
Swim with dolphins in the shiny sea
Underneath the starry night,
Go bungee-jumping off a mountain.

Fleur Watson (9)
Mayfield Primary School, Cambridge

The Magic Box

(Based on 'Magic Box' by Kit Wright)

I will put in my box . . .
The smell of sizzling bacon
The sound of dogs barking
And the sound of raindrops falling

I will put in my box . . .
The fuzzy hills of Scotland
The cooling seas of Croatia
And the green grass of the fields

I will put in my box . . .
My warm bed
The soft red sofa
The fun feeling of laughter

I will put in my box . . .
A dragon's scale
And a red pine cone

My box is made of . . .
Simple bronze
With red leather inside

In my box I will . . .
Fly like a bird.

Robin Macdonald (9)
Mayfield Primary School, Cambridge

Magic Box Poem

(Based on 'Magic Box' by Kit Wright)

I will put in my box . . .
A sound of a cat in the night
The smell of a jasmine swaying in the breeze

I will put in my box . . .
The sight of a cat sleeping
New York, a very busy place

I will put in my box . . .
My friend Mara
My friend Sophie
My friend Fleur
And my friend Phoebe

I will put in my box . . .
A magical ring
And a blue crumbling crystal

My box is made out of . . .
Red rubies and white diamonds

I will put in my box . . .
Some glittering white snow
And shining bright dolphins.

Neha Aggarwal (8)
Mayfield Primary School, Cambridge

A Magic Box Poem

(Based on 'Magic Box' by Kit Wright)

I will put in my box . . .
The smell of the nicest pizza in the world,
The sound of my silly billy dog,
The sound of silence in the night.

I will put in my box . . .
The sight of my dog sleeping,
The lovely sight of the big roller coaster in Disney Land,
The lovely sight of people cycling in Holland.

I will put in my box . . .
The feeling of a big sad cat in the distance,
My loving sister Eliza,
My best friend Neha.

I will put in my box . . .
A big puppet,
A massive unicorn in my house.

My box is made of . . .
Jewels with gold, silver and bronze,
In my box I love to swim with the lovely silky sleek dolphins.

Alice Hembrow (8)
Mayfield Primary School, Cambridge

Magic Box Poem

(Based on 'Magic Box' by Kit Wright)

I will put in my magic box . . .
The sound of the waves crashing from the ocean
The smell of the dry, smooth sand

I will put in my magic box . . .
The sight of the singing bird to the Australian desert
And Greenland's iceberg

I will put in my magic box . . .
The feeling of the angriest teacher shouting at me
I will put in my box . . .
The runner from the Olympic race

I will put in my box . . .
The fiery breath of the dragon
And the beautiful mermaid

My box is made of diamonds for the legs
And dragon's teeth for the lid

In my box I will play on the hot beach
And sail the seven seas.

Francesca Morelli (8)
Mayfield Primary School, Cambridge

My Holiday Haiku

I went to Egypt,
We stayed in a big hotel,
Back home on Sunday!

Lauren Roads (10)
Monks Risborough CE School, Princes Risborough

Snake

Smooth sliding snake
Dark diamond patterns
Camouflaged in the leaves and grass
Hissing as it moves
It stalks its prey

Its fangs are like freezing icicles
Its tongue is long and forked
Flicking out of the side of its mouth with hunger
It sees the plump rat and starts to dribble
Getting ready to swallow it whole

The rat escapes but the snake won't give up
It tries again
Sliding and gliding in the long grass
Its jaws open wide, its tongue flickers
In a flash the rat is gone

Head first the rat disappears
The snake's neck bulges
It doesn't bother to chew, it just swallows
The rat's tail slips down the snake's throat
The snake returns to its nest to rest.

Dominic Pavlopoulos (9)
Monks Risborough CE School, Princes Risborough

There Was . . . Limerick

There was a lady from Spain
Who loved to travel by train
She went to Geneva
But no one believed her
So she travelled back again.

Thomas Lidington (9)
Monks Risborough CE School, Princes Risborough

Why?

Why do you tell me off all the time?
Why do we have rules?
Why do you keep on yelling?
Why do we have to go in the school hall?

Why can't we wear home clothes?
Why do we have to do spellings?
Why don't you answer me?
Why do you keep on yelling?

Why do we have to do homework?
Why is this so boring?
Why can't we run around in the classroom?
Why can't we keep on drawing?
Why?

Amy Lipyeart (9)
Monks Risborough CE School, Princes Risborough

My Pet Alien

For my birthday I got a small, fluffy dog,
As it grew, so did my suspicions,
Its wagging tail was OK but sideways,
Flicking eyelids were another matter,
The family did not notice a thing.

His eyes glowed green in the night,
I begged to get rid of him but my family said, 'No, why?
You should appreciate your present. He's cute!'

One gloomy night I saw the eerie glow
And well, in the morning there was no sister,
I looked at my dog and threw it out . . .

Sean Hinton (9)
Monks Risborough CE School, Princes Risborough

Froggy

There once was a froggy sitting in a tree,
When a fly asked him, 'Will you please help me?'

The froggy didn't answer, the froggy didn't care,
As he was a vegetarian that froggy sitting there.

So he just sat there and sat there, day and night,
But when the fly flew home, he got a little fright!

As the sun went away and the froggy was alone,
An owl came behind him and took the froggy home.

Then out of the darkness came a short scuffle
And a baby owl came out in a sort of shuffle.

He ate that froggy there he did, he ate that froggy there
And when he had finished, he spat out froggy's hair.

That was the end of the froggy sitting in a tree,
When a fly asked him, 'Will you please help me?'

Charlie Walker (10)
Monks Risborough CE School, Princes Risborough

But I Love My Bed

The alarm goes off,
But I love my bed.

It's time to get up,
But I love my bed.

Mum's calling me,
But I love my bed.

I can smell pancakes cooking,
But I love my bed.

No! I love pancakes more.

Matthew Zelmanowicz (9)
Monks Risborough CE School, Princes Risborough

The Seaside

The sun blazing at the seashore,
Golden sand, gentle waves,
People sitting in their deckchairs,
Children paddling in the sea,
Seaweed round their feet,
Some building sandcastles,
Others exploring rock pools,
Gentle breezes, flying kites,
Summer holidays are *the best.*

Danielle Rolfe (9)
Monks Risborough CE School, Princes Risborough

The Environment

I can see the swaying of the leaves
And the raindrops dropping on the trees.
I can see the petals on the flowers scattering from the breeze.
I can hear the howling wind
And the rain splattering in the squidgy mud.
I can hear the pecking of the woodpecker on the tree,
I can feel the rain crashing on my face
And the mud crackling under my feet.
Then silence, all I can hear is the pecking of the birds.

Jamie-Lee Brooker (10)
Monks Risborough CE School, Princes Risborough

Poor Him Cinquain

The man,
He was so ill,
I felt sorry for him,
He was pale, not a bit of red,
Poor him.

Coral Morgan (10)
Monks Risborough CE School, Princes Risborough

Art Shirt That Was A Best Shirt

I was once a man's best shirt,
That went to all the parties and meetings,
Led a happy and joyful life,
Until the day I was given to the man's son.

Now I am an art shirt, getting mucky and dirty,
Sloshed with paint and chalks and other messy things,
I live a sad and sorry life, full of disappointment.

James Myerson (9)
Monks Risborough CE School, Princes Risborough

Range Rover Limerick

There once was a man from Dover,
Who bought a rusty Range Rover,
He thought it was nice,
To go sliding on ice,
But the car just rolled over and over.

George Moran (9)
Monks Risborough CE School, Princes Risborough

Quad Bike Race Cinquain

Quad bike
Get it going
We're going to go fast
Today we will be champions
Let's go.

Oliver Kamperis (10)
Monks Risborough CE School, Princes Risborough

The Beach

We're going to the beach,
With six pence each.
I can see birds coming down to land,
Now they are walking on the sand.

I can see the sea,
This is the place for me.
Look there's a boat!
Will it sink or will it float?

I'm in the sun,
Having a lot of fun.

Can I have an ice cream?
I'm really rather keen.
I like to explore the caves,
I like to jump the waves.

We enjoy collecting shells,
And listening to all the yells.
I can see people lying on their mats,
Fanning themselves with their hats.

I'm in the sun,
Having a lot of fun.

Although it's very hot,
I'm enjoying myself a lot.
I've found a rock pool,
And I dip my toes in, nice and cool!

We're watching a show,
While the sun is getting low.
The beach for me,
Is the place to be.

I'm in the sun,
Having a lot of fun!

Sarah Smart (10)
Monks Risborough CE School, Princes Risborough

My T-Rex

I have a pet T-Rex,
He really is so cool,
He lets me ride on his back
And sometimes comes to school.

But one day he wanted to explore,
So off he went to pack
And set off happily to London,
What's he doing? Come back!

He jumped over the Houses of Parliament
And terrified the Queen,
The police tried to chase him,
They can be quite mean.

He swam the English Channel
And ended up in France,
Dodged the Eiffel Tower
And did a little dance.

So then he went to Portugal
And got extremely hot,
He used gallons of suncream,
It must have cost a lot.

And then he went to the North Pole,
To try and cool off,
But snow went down his throat
And he caught a nasty cough.

So he decided to come back home
And had a jolly good nap,
He told us all about it
And showed us on the map.

Emily Brundrett (10)
Monks Risborough CE School, Princes Risborough

Skiing

I'm going away,
On a skiing holiday,
Very soon this year.
The aeroplane's ready,
But take it steady,
In a little while we'll be there.

It's a very long ride
And it's cloudy outside,
I hope it doesn't rain there.
Now the sun is shining,
My brother is whining,
But at least we are now here.

Skiing down,
The snowy ground,
Flashing past so quick.
Into the trees,
As quick as I please,
I really hope I don't trip!

Today's the day,
We end our holiday,
I enjoyed being here.
We had lots of fun,
Skiing in the sun,
We'll surely come back next year!

Marcus Nielsen (10)
Monks Risborough CE School, Princes Risborough

The Day I Got Abducted By Aliens

They say they don't exist,
They say there's no one out there.
But how come I saw a spaceship,
Just hovering in the air?

Then a light appeared through a hole in the ship
And it pulled me up like a shot.
A second later I found myself
In an alien cooking pot.

I clambered out of the rusty old pot
And came face to face with a guard.
With nasty green and mottled skin
And a face like a lump of lard.

With a yell I jumped in an air pipe
And started crawling like mad.
At last I could breathe again,
Not to be caught, I felt very glad.

At last I found the hole in the ship
And dropped through it with a sigh
And landed in my own fireplace,
Which luckily wasn't alight.

I crept out onto the hearth rug,
Had anyone noticed me leave?
Apparently Mum had not for she said,
'Go and wash your hands for tea.'

Barnaby Matthews (9)
Monks Risborough CE School, Princes Risborough

The Goal Haiku

The goalie dived right
The goal net billowed wildly
What a superb shot!

Conor Walker (9)
Monks Risborough CE School, Princes Risborough

Anger

Anger is red like the last balloon pops.
Anger sounds like a growling bear.
Anger tastes like boiling tea.
Anger smells like burning toast.
Anger looks like your house is on fire.
Anger feels like missing the plane.
Anger reminds me of the smashed china cup.

Lukmaan Jabar (10)
Oak Green School, Aylesbury

Sadness

Sadness is red like roses
Sadness sounds like someone crying
Sadness tastes like bitter
Sadness smells like lavender
Sadness looks like an eye watering
Sadness feels like heartbreak
Sadness reminds me of crying.

Desmond Mujana (9)
Oak Green School, Aylesbury

Anger

Anger is red like a hot, boiling tub of water
Anger sounds like a tiger roaring at me
Anger tastes like a hot cup of tea
Anger smells like something hot in your nose
Anger looks like a red devil standing in front of you
Anger feels like hot fire
Anger reminds me of a boy hitting me.

Sarfaraz Saghir (10)
Oak Green School, Aylesbury

Happiness

Happiness is yellow like the sun
Happiness sounds like butterflies
Happiness tastes like a mouthful of bananas
Happiness smells like flowers
Happiness looks like shiny gold
Happiness feels like the breezes
Happiness reminds me of golden eagles.

Lauren Byrne (9)
Oak Green School, Aylesbury

Happy

Happy is the rainbow painted in the sky,
It sounds like flowers shooting up from the soil,
It feels like you're the best,
It tastes like lovely strawberry cake,
It looks like the beautiful sunset,
It smells like fresh air,
It reminds me of my birthday.

Tabassum Naeem (9)
Oak Green School, Aylesbury

Sadness

Sadness is when you hear a person cry.
Sadness is when someone dies.
Sadness is when a family breaks up.
Sadness can never be something you're proud of.
Sadness is when it hurts.

Hallid Mahmood (9)
Oak Green School, Aylesbury

Anger

Anger is red like a tomato.
Anger sounds like a tomato popping.
Anger tastes like a red pepper.
Anger smells like petrol.
Anger looks like a heart cracking.
Anger feels like me being naughty.
Anger reminds me of a bull charging at me.

Tyler May (9)
Oak Green School, Aylesbury

Happiness

Happiness is pink like flowers from the garden,
It sounds like children playing together,
It tastes like lemon cake,
It smells like freshly-cut red roses,
It looks like fluffy kittens,
It feels like cuddling my teddy bear,
It reminds me of seeing my sister.

Holly Revell (10)
Oak Green School, Aylesbury

Fear

Fear's colour is black like darkness.
Fear sounds like thunder and lightning.
Fear tastes like having no one there.
Fear smells like getting shouted at.
Fear looks like being alone.
Fear feels like I should have not done that.
Fear reminds me I am alone.

Haroon Humzah (10)
Oak Green School, Aylesbury

Anger

What is anger?
Anger feels like no other feeling
Like you want to burst out and fight
You don't care who you fight with
Anger's a box you have to get out of
You don't care if anyone's out there
Anger is hot
Anger is red like a scorching sun
Anger you hate
Sometimes there's anger you control
But mainly anger nobody likes
Anger feels like you're not whole
That's what anger is.

Georgia Crane (9)
Oak Green School, Aylesbury

Angry

Angry is redder than my blood
It sounds like I want to fight with a rhino
Angry feels like I am going to burst
It smells very vicious like a lion's roar
It tastes like lava
It looks like me fighting
Angry reminds me of my parents shouting.

Morgan McCarthy (8)
Oak Green School, Aylesbury

Happy

Happy is when the sun shines,
Sounds like children laughing,
Feels like bubbles bursting,
Tastes like chicken nuggets,
Looks like smiling faces.

Connor Hennigan (7)
Oak Green School, Aylesbury

Sadness

Sadness is blue like someone crying.
Sadness sounds like raindrops splashing in a stream.
Sadness tastes like a ball of fire going down your throat.
Sadness smells like burning fire in your face.
Sadness looks like someone in the corner and doesn't
want to come out.
Sadness feels like a sword going through your brain.
Sadness reminds me of blue streams.

Luke Bright (9)
Oak Green School, Aylesbury

Surprised

Surprised is orange,
Surprised sounds like you've done something wrong,
Surprised feels shocking,
Surprised tastes like a creamy hot, hot, hot chocolate,
Surprised is pleasant,
Surprised smells like a chocolate-covered doughnut,
Surprised reminds me of when I broke my arm.

Kathryn Dixon (8)
Oak Green School, Aylesbury

Happy

Happy is like enjoyable fun.
Sounds like my little sister calling me.
Feels like a yellow sunshine shining on me.
Tastes like fish and chips from the seaside.
Looks like a bright yellow daffodil.

Jasmine Street (8)
Oak Green School, Aylesbury

Happy

Happy is silver and gold like the stars and moon.
It sounds like the birds singing the morning chorus.
It feels like you're playing with all your friends.
It smells like the fresh air all around.
It reminds me of all the happy times with my friends.
It makes me realise all the happy and sad times,
But best of all are the happy times.

Rikki Jones (9)
Oak Green School, Aylesbury

Confused

Confused is white with black swirls in the middle.
Confused sounds like owls hooting in my head.
Confused feels like someone has brainwashed me.
Confused tastes like a sour apple.
Confused looks like a colossal question mark.
Confused smells like paper.
Confused reminds me of trains.

Joe Craig (9)
Oak Green School, Aylesbury

Embarrassed

Embarrassed is when I go all red
It sounds like being laughed at
It feels like you have done something wrong
It looks like you are empty inside
It smells like the wind
It reminds me of the times I went bright red.

Danielle Webb (8)
Oak Green School, Aylesbury

Happy

Happy is excitement
Sounds like two birds singing
Feels like playing football
Tastes like a fresh, fat, chocolate doughnut
With hundreds and thousands on the top
Looks like a blackbird flying over my head
Smells like juicy, fat biscuits
Reminds me of singing with friends.

Daltan Taylor (9)
Oak Green School, Aylesbury

Love

Love is red like a heart
Love sounds like a night on a town
Love tastes like kissing somebody
Love smells like a sunny day
Love looks like romance
Love feels like hugging somebody
Love reminds me of my first date.

Rheanne Gordon (9)
Oak Green School, Aylesbury

Angry

Angry makes me feel like I am going to explode.
It sounds like a bomb going off.
It tastes like a sour sweet.
It looks like a car exploding on my head.
It smells like a mouldy banana.
It reminds me like my head's going to blow up.

Callum Jones (9)
Oak Green School, Aylesbury

Sadness

Sadness is black.
Sadness sounds like rain.
Feels like a shock of thunder.
Sadness tastes bitter.
Sadness looks like . . .
Sadness smells like burnt toast.
Sadness feels like I'm sinking deeper in the sea.
Sadness reminds me of when my nan was ill.

Billy Rogers (9)
Oak Green School, Aylesbury

Love

Love is pink like a row of hearts flowing all around you.
It sounds like birds humming to you sweetly.
It smells like a packet of hearts.
It tastes like strawberry ice cream fresh from the freezer.
It looks like people all around just cuddling.
It reminds me of my mum hugging me.

Paige Stevenson (8)
Oak Green School, Aylesbury

Happy

Happy is fun and cool, like me
It sounds like kids playing in the park
It feels like jumping on the biggest trampoline in the world
It tastes like the biggest, chocolatey cake in the world
It looks like all the colours of the rainbow.

Macauley Stott (9)
Oak Green School, Aylesbury

Laughter

Laughter is blue like a swimming pool
It sounds like me when I am being tickled
It feels like people playing in a park
It tastes like chocolate in my mouth
It looks like a fair with loads of candy
It smells like my nan baking a cake
It reminds me of my holiday in Devon.

Georgia Adams (8)
Oak Green School, Aylesbury

Darkness

Darkness is red like blood in the water.
It sounds like lava exploding out of a volcano.
It feels like people being tortured.
It tastes like fresh blood from an animal.
It looks like people being killed.
It smells like an old granny's house.
It reminds me of my baby cousin kicking and screaming.

Elliot Riley (8)
Oak Green School, Aylesbury

Anger

Anger is red like a red chilli.
It sounds like thunder in cold weather.
It feels like being angry.
It tastes like Brussels.
It looks like a red nasty monster.
It smells like nasty mud and worms.
It reminds me of being very, very angry.

Shannon Woolhead (8)
Oak Green School, Aylesbury

Hunger

Hunger is black like an empty hole.
It tastes like an empty packet of crisps.
It sounds like your tummy rumbling.
It looks like burnt pine.
It sounds like death.
It feels like somebody beating me.
It smells like McDonald's when you have no money.
It reminds me of a big Christmas dinner.

Alisha Bruno (8)
Oak Green School, Aylesbury

Hope

Hope is blue like a sunny summer's day.
It sounds like birds singing at dawn.
It feels like a baby sleeping soundly.
It tastes like a strange cake that I have never tried before.
It looks like a country with nothing else but candy.
It smells like fresh bread straight from the oven early in the morning.
It reminds me of puppies and kittens playing in the snow.

Courtney Green (9)
Oak Green School, Aylesbury

Anger

Anger is red like a bull charging
It sounds like flashing thunder
It feels like hot boiling water
It tastes like bubbling hot lava
It looks like a mad bull charging
It smells like my nasty sister
It reminds me of my naughty friend.

William Ginn (9)
Oak Green School, Aylesbury

Love

Love is purple like my favourite sweet.
It smells like the waves of the sea.
It looks like a man picking fresh roses for a woman.
It tastes like sweets of different colours.
It feels like the waves splashing on the beach.
It sounds like a woman talking to a man.
It reminds me of my dad.

Megan Brown (8)
Oak Green School, Aylesbury

Hate

Hate is red like lava bubbling.
It sounds like red thunder.
It feels like bones are crushing.
It tastes like disgusting medicine.
It looks like a fire that never goes out.
It smells like black smoke.
It reminds me of fresh blood.

Otis Roberts (9)
Oak Green School, Aylesbury

Fun

Fun is light blue like a big wave.
It sounds like the sea rustling in my ear straight at me.
It feels like a warm ray from the sunny sky.
It tastes like lots of sweets melting in my mouth.
It looks like lots of little children playing games.
It smells like flowers freshly picked.
It reminds me of my kind dad.

Lucy Sprowell (8)
Oak Green School, Aylesbury

Love

Love is orangey-red like a heart thumping
It sounds like birds singing on the tree trunks
It feels like dancing with love
It tastes like strawberry milkshake
It looks like kissing each other
It smells like fresh blue water
It reminds me of my auntie in Pakistan.

Nazish Abbas (9)
Oak Green School, Aylesbury

Love

Love is red like a mini motor.
It sounds like people singing.
It feels lovely and warm.
It tastes like strawberries.
It looks like happy people.
It smells like flowers.
It reminds me of playing on my PlayStation.

Rafael Rebelo-Miranda (9)
Oak Green School, Aylesbury

Happiness

Happiness is like a bath full of roses.
It sounds like beautiful singers singing on a stage.
It tastes like biting into a big choccie.
It looks like a big hippopotamus swimming gleefully in the water.
It feels like a teddy hugging my heart.
It reminds me of my beautiful family.

KC Franceschini (9)
Oak Green School, Aylesbury

Happiness

Happiness is like a nice sunny day.
It sounds like a laughing cheetah.
It tastes like a chocolate.
It looks like your heart breaking into happiness.
It feels like you're singing into happiness.
It reminds me of being in Pakistan.

Amber Nasreen (9)
Oak Green School, Aylesbury

Anger

Anger is like a volcano bursting out.
It sounds like somebody ripping out your heart.
It tastes like the hottest thing you could ever taste.
It looks like a devil staring at you right in the eye.
It feels like me standing in an oven.
It reminds me of my best friend betraying me.

Abbie Osborne (9)
Oak Green School, Aylesbury

Happiness

Happiness is as yellow as the sandy beach.
It sounds like a little bird singing.
It tastes like the first lick of an ice cream.
It looks like the fun of the fair.
It feels like a butterfly on your skin.
It reminds me of my dad.

Ieva Pakalniskyte (9)
Oak Green School, Aylesbury

Happiness

Happiness is like butterflies all over you.
It sounds like music pumping in your head.
It tastes like a cup of water thrown inside your mouth.
It looks like a sandy beach with yellow sand.
It feels like a hot warm sun on top of you.
It reminds me of when I was first born.

Chelsea Davies (9)
Oak Green School, Aylesbury

Anger

Anger is red like fire
It sounds like a roaring, exploding volcano
It feels like steam coming out of my ears
It tastes like red bubbly lava in a cauldron
It smells like fierce burning lava
It reminds me of my sly sister.

Jade Street (8)
Oak Green School, Aylesbury

Fear

Fear is black like a really dark night
It sounds like a wolf making weird noises
It tastes like a ghost ripping out my heart
It looks like a black bubble with vampires inside them
It feels like fear growing in my heart
It reminds me of my worst nightmare.

Mohammed Aftab (9)
Oak Green School, Aylesbury

Happiness

Happiness is yellow like the sun shining down on me.
It tastes like a pizza with lots of extra toppings.
It sounds like a bird singing a happy tune.
It looks like golden daffodils waving their heads in the sun.
It feels like the sea tickling my feet.
It reminds me of the feel of the sandy beach.

Amber Whitney (9)
Oak Green School, Aylesbury

Fear

Fear is black like the scary night.
It sounds like an owl hooting in flight.
It tastes like something mouldy from out of a tree.
It looks like something out of 'Scary Movie 3'.
It feels like something taking you to their lair.
It reminds me of my worst nightmare.

Lucy Warwick (9)
Oak Green School, Aylesbury

Happy

Happy is when all my family get together for a special day out.
It sounds like all my family love me.
It tastes like melted chocolate that makes my taste buds water.
It looks like all my family are all there beside me all the time.

Leah Clayton-Temple (9)
Oak Green School, Aylesbury

Happiness

Happiness is yellow like you've bought an ice cream.
It sounds like the sand.
It tastes like an ice cream.
It looks like my hair.
It feels like my love.
It reminds me of my bird singing.

Hannah Baldwin (9)
Oak Green School, Aylesbury

Bill

There was a young boy called Bill
Who lived on the top of a hill
He went out one day
And got blown away
And Bill ended up at the mill!

Luke Murphy (10)
Priory School, Prittlewell

Kelly

There was a young girl called Kelly
Who sometimes wore a welly
She didn't want to get wet
So she made a bet
With her brother who was watching telly.

Jordan Needs (10)
Priory School, Prittlewell

Whiskers Gnashman

Whiskers Gnashman, gnashes through wooden dwellings
Gnash!
>*Gnash!*
>>*Gnash!*
Looking for Red Leicester to make his favourite dinner
Toasted apple and cheese pie!
Lazy is his attitude
He reads newspapers, which are always by his side,
After lazy mode he runs swiftly
Swifter,
>*Swifter,*
>>*Swifter,*
Getting on his jacket, jumps down the road to the sharpening house
Quickly goes to get to the local church
To gnaw through the main supports and his dirty work!
Still he isn't too happy . . .
For he only has one ear!

Owen Rees (9)
St Helen's Primary School, Ipswich

The Pied Piper's Poem

The piper loves his rich chocolate-brown pipe
Which has magic notes.
He shows off his glittery golden eyes
While the sun shines brightly on his warm, long, curved hat.
Roar! He has a temper like a dinosaur, which doesn't get him far.
He has a wavy gown made of beautiful silk.
One song from his magical pipe
Would make you want to get up and dance.
Tip tap tip tap, he creeps along the ground
With the rats following behind.
Hooray, the rats have gone away!

Louie Bloom (8)
St Helen's Primary School, Ipswich

Pied Piper

Pied Piper the piper,
Battles with his gleaming pipe
While he finds his
Special Tudor Rose cloak
He is a very active person so if you
Want some magic
You'll have to book!
Until the moon sleeps, you'll
See a *shine*
In-between his
Suspicious conker-brown eyes
You'll always be *amused*
By his sense of humour
Some days he is annoying
Other days he is a lovely person!
Piper is a man
Who loves to impress,
But how he keeps on going
I just don't know!

Francesca Cross (9)
St Helen's Primary School, Ipswich

The Pied Piper's Poem!

The pied piper, a jolly lad, pipes every town at carnival nights
Crumpa-crumpa clatters his do-decahedron hat
You will hear him, each night piping his tune.
His pipe is a wonder; music pops like a blazing balloon
Feather is a pentagon, very neatly kept, like a sacred amulet.
Eyes like a staring eagle, ears like a water lily
Never brushes his magnolia teeth.
People approach from side to side, to hear his tune.

When the piper in the moonlit night, has a gleeful sleep.

Pratik Bikkannavar (9)
St Helen's Primary School, Ipswich

The Rats In Hamelin Town

Rats! Rats! Everywhere!
Hideous ugly shoe brushes
Scrambling around our small town.

All they are is grimy lumps of fur
Why don't they leave us alone?

Their tails are like salmon cobras
Swaying in the wind.

Always dropping litter
In the villagers' gardens.

We loathe rodents
In our town this place is as small
As a crumb of a ginger nut biscuit

Everyone wishes they a-packing to Greece.

Carlie Osborne (8)
St Helen's Primary School, Ipswich

Playground Children!

Jump and scream aloud
Children munching tasty crisps
Play games with your friends.

Boys playing football
Kicking the ball to the goal
Oh no! Missed the net.

Bullies come and join
Moving backwards and forwards
Whistle blows, in time.

Afsana Islam (11)
St Helen's Primary School, Ipswich

Pied Piper's Poem

My boastful manner can get annoying after a while
I can be jolly but I don't very much like it.
I play my pipe with its magic b flat
Very busy in my life
I never have time to stop.
Busy, busy, busy,
I'm also very clever, helpful too . . . poetic I can be.
I like to get things done.
I get vexed at people like the mayor
He never keeps his promise.
I like to pose . . . I'm arty too.
I get really lively when I'm near *you*
My language is quite formal
I'm exciting when I see children
Very fair, I am changeable too!
Splash!
The rats are in the river!

Ottillie Cook (8)
St Helen's Primary School, Ipswich

Poseidon

P ollution he hates
O cean he loves
S ea is not his enemy
E vil to fish he hates
I n the sea he might be
D olphins love him
O cean he owns
N ever will he hate the sea.

Tiffany Evripidou (8)
St Helen's Primary School, Ipswich

The Pied Piper

Got a magical pipe.
If flows like a river
Trousers as shiny as glitter.
Catches rats
Shows off.

Tall hat
Went to Hamelin town.

Who could he be?
He loves his pipe.

Dresses in moon shadow-blue clothes
Cloak, soft as a newborn chick
Lively!
Shines in the sunlight.
Skips across everywhere!

Looks down on the dusty floor
Looking for rats.

Who could he be?

Was really joyful, suddenly . . .
Gets cross-fierce.

Sometimes can be a weirdo.

Always doing poses thinking he's the best
Who could he be?

Do you know?

H-e-'s t-h-e Pied Piper!

Yiuk-Ngor To (8)
St Helen's Primary School, Ipswich

Fur Face The Rat

Fur Face, the furry fat rat who wears a coat of stinky,
smelly chestnut fur,
Feeds on the garbage from a dump
But his favourite thing to do is to chew and gnaw oak.
It is unfortunate that one of Fur Face's ears is cut off
But the other one is as bright
As rosy-red roses.
R&B music is what he listens to
Especially 'Ratinem'.
Royal purple eyes
Like rainforests Fur Face has got.
He doesn't swim
In swimming pools but in the stinking smelly sewers,
Very often Fur Face
Uses slang words like 'Innit'.

Isabella Carrino (9)
St Helen's Primary School, Ipswich

Screaming Madness Haiku

Children are screaming
Petrified, screeching children
Fear in the playground.

Boys scaring the girls
Children screaming, having fun
When I'm playing games.

I play with my friends
Bell goes off when I'm playing
Time to come in now.

Emily Clarke-Beard (10)
St Helen's Primary School, Ipswich

Dozey Toes The Cat

Strange things have been happening in Hamelin . . .
Things like bitter-tasting ants scurry through my fur.
I'd rather be playing with tassels
Counting my curvy claws.
The stinky sewer swimmers try to 'cat' my attention,
Never will they annoy me
I dream as if I am a platinum kite tail,
Swinging from side to side!

In 'dis' catty club I'm the . . .
Coolest, the best and the grubbiest of them all
Me, Dozey Toes, am a ball of string trundling through the street.
Oh yes - strange things have been happening
In Hamelin and there always will be . . .

Beckie Fiddaman (9)
St Helen's Primary School, Ipswich

Sleepy Peeper

Sleepy Peeper, the lazy ginger cat
Dreams of flying with the birds,
Tap, tap, her little feet go when she walks across the path.
You will see her sleepwalk at midnight,
And when Sleepy Peeper goes out at night to party,
She puts paint on her face instead of make-up,
When she slithers along,
Her tail flaps side to side like a vibrating snake,
Slowly she falls asleep and dreams about flying with the birds.
Strangely she still sleeps and dreams
Of flying with the birds to this very day.

Ellie Goodwin (9)
St Helen's Primary School, Ipswich

Red Leicester

Red Leicester
The tangy
Orange rat.
His nose is a grey pin.
He's got quadrilateral feet.
Tingly-tangly tail which wraps round cheese.
Counting money in the night, while in the day watching TV.

He's got cheesy whiskers from outer space.

His teeth can gnaw through metal
His teeth are pierced
Which he can bite through the metal with
Rats are everywhere.

Jacob Buckley (9)
St Helen's Primary School, Ipswich

Colours Of Beauty!

The first thing I see when I trot out the door is colours,
Trees are green and golden brown,
Clothes are blue, green and pink,
They wrap around the children like vines of a tree.
Playground in beauty I've seen it today,
It's down to the colour, that's what I say.
A shirt that's red fire, a bright silver token,
A huge, great big snowball, now probably broken.

So who would ban colours?
Not me.

Thomas Powell (9)
St Helen's Primary School, Ipswich

Dirty Rat's Tale

Death, beautiful *death* is my game.
My soft angora fur is a disaster everywhere.
I'm a sewer scavenger
I've got football stud claws.
Plague, plague, and plague, I love it so!
I steal so much money.
I've got no shadow
I'm a gangster man.

I love human fire-red blood
I'm a beer gluggin' rat
I lost two claws
I've got moonlight bay eyes
I'm so poisonous.

As soon as my claws come back . . .
I will be king again!
Move it!

Jake Templeton (8)
St Helen's Primary School, Ipswich

Playtime Haiku

The girls start to play
I hear lots of loud screaming
I talk to people.

I see my friends play
Boys are kicking the football
The girls are skipping.

Shhh! Whistle has gone
All the children stand quiet
Then they all line up.

Stacey Walker (9)
St Helen's Primary School, Ipswich

Lunchtime!

Crazy colours filling the playground
The munching, crunching sound of the crisps.
Children are pouncing wild springs.
Girls moving and grooving
Lonely children drooping their heads,
Wanting to drift back to their classroom.
Teachers and children sinking their teeth into mouth-watering snacks
Grinning adults sipping their drinks,
Lively children scattering to the fresh water fountain
In the fruit bin lays lazy skins
People hanging around for their school dinner letter to come up
Cheering,
'Another letter!
Not ours!
Oooh! My tummy is rumbling!'
Children, like cheetahs,
Sprinting out of packed lunch, ready to play
Suddenly the shriek of the whistle!
'Oh, no!
Maybe next play!'

Bethany Durrant (9)
St Helen's Primary School, Ipswich

Playtime Panic

Playtime starts at ten
Playground panic spreads throughout
Playtime finishes.

Lunch brings joy to all
You can see the huge football!
Stop! No more football.

They make a big mess
I tidy the messy hall
All back to normal.

Brennan Butler (11)
St Helen's Primary School, Ipswich

The Big Fat Bully Haiku

The big fat bully
Is here; oh no, not me too!
He always brings fear.

I try to run off
He calls me horrible names
When I play my games.

Time for the whistle
Glad to go back in to school
When play is over.

Tanatswa Kazangarare (9)
St Helen's Primary School, Ipswich

Violin

V olume up
I t's E string
O h so high
L et's play it again
I t might be better
N ow play on!

Paul Armitage (7)
St Helen's Primary School, Ipswich

Athena

A thens was named after Athena
T hey grew olives on the trees
H er brain was very quick
E very evil enemy she hated
N ight-time owls were her symbols
A thena loved art.

Tansie Shoults (7)
St Helen's Primary School, Ipswich

Dozey Toes The Cat

Strange things have been happening in Hamelin town . . .

Rats are everywhere, scurrying up and down alleyways,
Nibbling rubbish, swimming in the sewers,
Spreading disease everywhere.
They are bitter-tasting ants, disgusting, very different flavours.
One climbed into my fur yesterday
With a big army trying to attack me!
But luckily I sneezed and they all flew off like birds!

I won't let them test my patience . . .
I'd rather be tapping a shining silver star . . .

Or sailing on one of those wooden planks
With a big bedding blanket to a faraway island
To find treasure like a pirate,
Have a parrot on my shoulder and wear a golden earring
You can try to make me catch rats
But the answer will always be . . .
'No!'

Hannie Phillips (8)
St Helen's Primary School, Ipswich

Playtime Haiku

Girls start to gossip
Boys are having fun playing
I talk to people.

We wait for our lunch
The cooks are making us lunch
Children eat their food.

Tummy full from lunch
Bellies can't run as fast now
I need to rest now.

Maggie Fielder (10)
St Helen's Primary School, Ipswich

Who Is He?

Cloak blows in the strong wind
Shining costume in the sun
The rats obey his commands.
Glowing costume all day long,
Struts along when he's playing the pipe.
He likes doing artistic poses.
Gets angry easily.
Long skinny legs and a very tall hat,
Drove the rats into the river
Little pipe twitters all day and night.
Angry when he didn't get his silver pieces
He moves as gracefully as a peacock
Cloak sways like peacocks feathers in the wind.
Big and strong,
Thinks he's the best.
Who is he?

Hannah Turner (9)
St Helen's Primary School, Ipswich

Playground Pleasure

When the bell goes you run out
Some start jumping,
Some start screaming,
I run over to play.
Thinking what a marvellous day.
Oh, there's my friends bouncing the ball,
If I run I hope I don't fall
It turns cold as the whistle blows,
Children's faces stop still
Everybody just
Freezes!

Kelsie Simmons (10)
St Helen's Primary School, Ipswich

Going In The Playground!

If you are feeling lonely,
Don't just sit there!
Go to the playground!
And ask a friend to come.
If you see a bully,
And he's troubling you.
Don't go away.
Be brave and make him,
Go away instead!
You can also play games,
Like football, cricket, or catch,
Until the playground closes.
Then you can come,
Another day!

Soham Dixit (9)
St Helen's Primary School, Ipswich

The Piper's Back

The piper is the man to be who he loves to be.
He loves to pose in front of the sunlight
He has the most precious pipe,
Also he has a silver and golden-coloured cloak.
The piper is the most popular man with his pipe.
The pipe sounds like a bird tweeting and swaying in the moonlight.
The pipe is a light red colour.
It has a lovely, gorgeous tune and a sweet little tweet,
He skips and topples when he plays
Everyone stares, as he never stops playing with it.
Its tune is the funniest tune that a little sometimes
Most of the time he has his gorgeous tune of a bird swaying
He loves to pose more than anyone else.

Imogen Milner (8)
St Helen's Primary School, Ipswich

The Lonely Loos

The loos are as smelly as my older brother
(And he's really smelly!)
People gobble their snack in there,
Not a good combination.

Some people hang around in there and chit chat
A few of the loos are surviving
But the rest are *'Out of order'*,
They're as old as my grandad!

How many people have sat on their seats?
Would you like it if you were them?
I bet they haven't been cleaned in years.

They have been standing there
For as long as anyone can remember!
They might be there, unchanged
Long after we've left!

Poor, ancient loos!

Amelia Cousins (10)
St Helen's Primary School, Ipswich

Athena

A thens was named after Athena
T he owl was her symbol
H elped good people
E nemies she hated
N obody was as clever as Athena
A nd she loved paintings.

Josef Bryant (7)
St Helen's Primary School, Ipswich

Defender

The ball screaming, people scoring a burnt-out goal
Strong place but not in the winter, strong people in the summer.
The ball is a coal-fired eye of lava red.
Keeper is the only one, every person depending on him.
The lump of coal, burning his kit,
Ripping his gloves, a sting on the hands.
Keeper saves it but on the ground.
Last defender in the way.
Bleeding legs, a river of fire pain.
Keeper's back, defender saves the day.
'Unstoppable!' the keeper would say.
The games at half, defender down!
They are more worried about him than the score.
Teachers run out to the playground.
A broken leg at least, headmaster taking him to the hospital.
The end of school
They play once and for all.
'What shall we do without him?' asked Jamie
'Who cares if we win or lose? It's just a game,' explained Matt.

Matthew Gorrard (10)
St Helen's Primary School, Ipswich

Hermes

H appy helpful god
E njoys delivering messages
R uns extremely fast
M essenger of the gods
E agle runner
S hoes striped with feathers on the back.

Tom Warburton (7)
St Helen's Primary School, Ipswich

Friends 4 Ever

Chatting, talking all day long
Best friends, other friends, any friends will do
Help me, like a teacher.
I don't know what I'd do without them
Hooray for friends!
Their heart is pure gold
Our life wouldn't be the same without them
Everyone needs a friend
Play exciting games with them
They don't leave you out.
True friends won't tell.
My friendship is pure.
Just like fresh apple juice
Friends only have little arguments . . .
If any
Secret magical handshakes
Keep things private
Maybe even a special language.
Do you like having friends?

Katie Pettican (10)
St Helen's Primary School, Ipswich

The Piper

He is proud of his face.
His cloak is as fluffy as a day-born chick.
He is like a mysterious myth.
His teeth are like the white clouds in the sky.
He can blow his pipe as fast as cheetah's legs.
His trousers are silkier than a spiderweb.
His clothes are as bright as a new rainbow.
His boots are as precious as a wedding ring.

Iqbal Ali (9)
St Helen's Primary School, Ipswich

Children Go Wild

Children running around like runner beans
Crashing into each other, bumps, bruises, nasty red sticky stuff
It's mayhem!
Teachers trying to stop them, but they've turned into lions
The scary head teacher comes out, the children run and hide.
It's gone silent!
But one stays out, he says,
'I'm all alone and I've got a feeling I'm in deep, deep trouble.'
All I can hear is the sound of a saxophone,
The head comes over I've back-chatted the head.
He phones my parents; I've got suspended.
All I can hear is my mum yelling
I'm not listening, I'm to busy thinking what I've done.
Mum sends me to my room.
I get out of the window into my tree house.
I sleep there for tonight at least.

Rhys Lucock (10)
St Helen's Primary School, Ipswich

Poseidon

P rotects all fish
O ver the sea
S ea is special to him
E vil to fish he hates
I n the sea he can be
D ominant over fish
O cean he owns
N ever lets fish down.

Jemima Hindmarch (8)
St Helen's Primary School, Ipswich

Ocean Wonders

The shark
Swiftly it glides through calm waters,
Slicing them in half with a razor blade tail,
Suddenly it strikes!

The dolphin,
As agile as an athlete, it loops through the blue,
Conversing in high-pitched whistles,
A diving angel.

The octopus,
Sneakily it hides in shipwrecks,
Snatching passing shellfish,
A black gangster.

The whale,
Slowly it floats through darkened waters
Vacuuming passing fish in to its huge mouth,
An ocean wonder.

The whirlpool,
Swirling, it sweeps up innocent fish,
Thrashing and ripping up lives,
Tearing baby fish from their parents,
Whizzing round and round as if hypnotised,
Finally, as the horror slows,
The calm waters carry limp and lifeless bodies,
They float to the golden beach!

Hal Rudkin (11)
St Helen's Primary School, Ipswich

Fun For Everyone

There's fun for everyone!
At lunch there's skipping ropes, tennis rackets,
Sponge balls and more.
The boys bring balls and play football
Most girls hang around and chat
The playground's on a slope,
So if you play netball the ball might go down the hill
The trees are fluffy logs which sway in the wind.
There's screaming and shouting
Muttering and whispering noise everywhere
The little ones are provided with fruit
While the older children bring crisps or fruit
There are so many different colours all over the playground,
Red, yellow, green, blue, black, white and lots more.
Have fun, it's worth it.

Rebecca Addison (9)
St Helen's Primary School, Ipswich

Playground Mayhem Haiku

Quiet as a mouse
The cool, smooth breeze blowing slow,
Nature stays the same.

The children run out
Shouting and screaming out loud
Running wild and free.

Then the loud bell goes
Noisy children go inside
Then nature comes back.

Aimee Prentice (9)
St Helen's Primary School, Ipswich

The Killer Coat

The killer coat can strangle you! Drown you! Crush you!
Its pockets eat up things inside them
Beware or it shall eat your hat and gloves with its razor mouth
The buttons turn to evil eyes and stare at you
The colour of it is blazing red so beware of that coat
One cold, snowy day in the playground
The red coat sneaked out of the cloakroom
And looked for a girl or boy to feed on.
But he could not choose
So he crept down the corridor but still could not choose.
On he went, looking for supper, when suddenly he had an idea.
He would eat all the girls and boys.
He ran into the classrooms and children screamed.
Teachers cried, 'I'll lose my job!'
But it was too late.
The red coat had already eaten up every single scrap
Of slimy supper.
So take my advice
Beware of that coat!

Jemima Senior (9)
St Helen's Primary School, Ipswich

Night-Time

' N ow is the time you go to bed,
 I t's 8 o'clock so' Mum said
 G ood dreams give good luck
 H ey it's total yuck!
 T ime out, I'll read a story.

 T he moon is up
 I t's not fair, I go to bed
 M um I wish you said,
 E mergency, I have to go to bed!

Georgie Fitch (7)
St Helen's Primary School, Ipswich

Mystery Guest

He threatens the village as he struts past
He flicks his golden locks
As the tunes come from the chestnut instrument
Does it come from his pipe?
That is a clue to his name!
Where did he come from?
Where has he been?
He pops up everywhere!
But . . . where has he gone?
What did he say?
He's mysterious
But he is the man who sent away the rats
And he is . . . the *piper!*

Maisie Clarke (9)
St Helen's Primary School, Ipswich

A Song About The Piper

A cloak ao fluffy as a day-born chick
He sprouts like a rainbow
As quick as a sparrow he moves,
The mystery poser
An outrageous hippy most definitely!
Struts about like he owns the place.
The hypnotised rats obey all orders.
A colossal man
Been in and out of countries
A mysterious man

He flows like the river of doom.
He whistles to the rats and they plunge into the river.

Ilya Cereso (9)
St Helen's Primary School, Ipswich

Weather

The sun is a calm and peaceful mind
Sleeping dreamily on a hilltop.

A storm is a raging human
Always in fights.

Thunder is a storming child
Running to their room.

The rain is a crying baby
Wanting more attention.

The wind is a snorting person
Prepared to defend its territory.

Snowflakes are flying angels
Swooping down from Heaven.

A rainbow is a smiling infant
Walking around with happiness.

Weather is a dangerous force but still amazing.

Rusharne Brown-Powell (10)
St Helen's Primary School, Ipswich

My Dad

My dad is a strong tree, which will live forever,
Quite peaceful like a small prickly hedgehog,
Crashing waves of the sea is my dad whistling,
And a red butterfly blooming is my dad singing.
He's a roaring lion, when he's angry and jealous
And is a chestnut puppy when he is sleeping
All the time, when he's working, the sound of a cat, purrs happily
But when he's bruised or smirking the sound of a dog is weeping.

Amber Durrant (11)
St Helen's Primary School, Ipswich

What Happens When My Teacher Gets Mad?

(You wouldn't want to know)
When my teacher gets mad,
He really gets mad,
He stomps his feet,
And his face turns cherry-red
He scrapes up his hair,
And wails out loud,
In a voice so icy,
My hair freezes in an instant,
He bangs the tables,
And hurls his possessions,
He puts his head in his arms,
And mumbles to himself.
That's what happens,
When my teacher gets mad.
(I told you that you wouldn't want to know.)

Sangeeta Kaur (11)
St Helen's Primary School, Ipswich

Playground Prance

Lessons over run outside,
Find our spot where we can
Dance with pride.

Oh no! Footballers are coming what can we do,
They tell us to go and say,
'Shoo, shoo, shoo.'

Rush for the corners,
Everyone squeezes in,

Whistle blows
Now play is over and everyone goes.

Mitzi Munuo (10)
St Helen's Primary School, Ipswich

Who Is It?

An artistic poser
Who could it be?
If he doesn't get his way
He will get a temper
He has a hat to make
Him have a big attitude.
Who could it be?
He has a pipe like silk,
Who could it be?
Cape flowing in the wind
A dolphin blue coat
Long legs and funny boots
Who could it be?
Clothes of the prettiest cloth
Who could it be?
Glides like a dove
Strides like a king
Who could it be?
Rhymes in his words
Who could it be?
Takes away the rats
With a little pipe
Who could it be?
Revenge seeker of Hamelin town
Who could it be?
Imaginary or real
Who could it be?
Guess
'It's the Pied Piper'
Hooray!

Grace Clarke (9)
St Helen's Primary School, Ipswich

Children's Paradise

Fabulous fresh fruit!
Beneath a huge orange rose,
Climb tall oaks,
Surrounded by water, garden, grass.
Hear sweet robins singing welcomes.
Paradise!

Mountains are thinking,
'What . . . sweet children!'
While crying glaciers of happiness.

Melancholy parents wailing
Tears of lavender,
Clutching teddies,
Longing for the return of their children.
Sadly, the tears of lavender caused the teddies to disintegrate.

Finn Rudkin (8)
St Helen's Primary School, Ipswich

Rushing For Play

Lessons have stopped
Everyone is rushing down
To have a great time.

Everyone is loud
Children are kicking about
Girls are screaming loud.

Stop! Whistle has gone
Children stand still with no noise
Everyone lined up.

Arm Sathuphap (11)
St Helen's Primary School, Ipswich

Tsunami

A destructive earthquake
Like an elephant stampede
A magnificent roar,
Out at sea,
A sign of death.

How does this happen?
Scientists know,
Smashing and crashing,
Buildings destroyed,
Water denominating,
Plates out of place,
Ruins as far as the eye sees,
Why?

Henrik Anderson (10)
St Helen's Primary School, Ipswich

War

Drums beating like a heartbeat,
Left, right, left, right,
Black shapes of death hurtling forward,
The army demolishing everything in their path,
Children being pulled in by mothers
Telling them everything's going to be alright
The warriors trudging past, no colour, no energy in their eyes.
The enemy a million spots in the distance.
Oh why, oh why can't they see it's wrong?
My last words,
'Please stop!'

Eleanor Turner (10)
St Helen's Primary School, Ipswich

My Mum

My mum is a peaceful afternoon,
She is a relaxing sea
She makes me go over the moon
She is a star to me.

My mum is a comfy armchair
She makes me cosy and cool
She never ever shouts at me,
She is not an empty stool.

My mum is tasty sugar,
Sweet but never bitter
She is a tidy room,
Never covered with litter.

Pashmina Bhutto (10)
St Helen's Primary School, Ipswich

In The Playground, That I Love!

The children as bright as the sun
The noise of thousands of gongs crashing
Together with anger and fear.
Children running like fire racing through the breezy air.
The lonely boy in the corner stands as still as stone.
His tears racing over the playground in a flood
Tears are power, power is blood!
Children telling their personal secrets to one another
Girls dancing as professional cheerleaders on the football pitch.
They're a ray of sunshine on a gloomy day!

Shakira Holder (9)
St Helen's Primary School, Ipswich

The Amazing Piper

A beautiful rainbow in the sky
When he leaps
He's a bit of a poser.
Who is he?
His cloak gleams when the sun shines on it.
Do you know who it is yet?
It is the Piper!
The pipe he has plays an amazing little tune.
His cloak floats like a leaf.

Russell Bye-Lewis (9)
St Helen's Primary School, Ipswich

The Pied Piper

His eyes glow of daylight,
Like a jolly elf,
Skipping through the forest giving spring to autumn.
As he passes, pleasure makes the sun shine brighter than before.

A prairie gold flute glistens,
Magical music pours out, putting all rats in a trance.
'Rats beware!' someone shouts
Getting closer - with *no* warning,
Splash! . . . As a high-pitched voice cries, 'The rats . . . are ruined!'

Holly Gooch (9)
St Helen's Primary School, Ipswich

Beach

B each is fun watching waves
E ating chips by the caves
A ll jump in . . . it's freezing cold
C ockles yum, I'm drinking rum!
H ey don't splash me!

Stanley Rudkin (7)
St Helen's Primary School, Ipswich

Playing A Football Match Haiku

Like to play football
There's a boy that's got the ball
He shoots and he scores.

He never misses
Hearing people practising
Enjoying themselves.

Another match now
Excitement scoring again
Whistle blows, match ends.

Youness Chemmaa (10)
St Helen's Primary School, Ipswich

Playtime Haiku

It is quiet now
It's the beginning of play
Everyone is here.

Jumping about now
The popping of crisp packets
Bang go the packets.

It is quiet now
It is the end of playtime
Everyone has gone.

Kayleigh Harris (10)
St Helen's Primary School, Ipswich

Greece

G reece had
R eally quite a big
E mpire
E lephants in the east
C rete was where it started. An
E xtraordinary volcano destroyed it.

Lily J Stewart (7)
St Helen's Primary School, Ipswich

My Dad

Beer-boozer
Rugby-lover
Paper-peruser
Job-juggler
Aftershave-user
Tall-looker
Housewife-helper
Active-worker
Shopping-minder
PlayStation-loser
Restaurant-buyer
Birthday-spender
Trouble-sorter
Homework-maker
Car-keeper.

Ellie Wells (11)
Spinfield School, Marlow

My Sister

Make-up wearer
Hair carer
Chocolate eater
Ball beater
Hockey player
Peace breaker
Test hater
Argument creator
Boy lover
Party recoverer
Toilet blocker
Bedroom locker
Keen jogger
Computer hogger.

Conor Monaghan (10)
Spinfield School, Marlow

My Cousin Isabel

Strong swimmer
Pink dresser
Attention seeker
Specs wearer
Scar bearer
Toy player
Trampoline lover
Thunderbird gamer
Diabetic resister
Injection loather
Television watcher.

George Barrett (10)
Spinfield School, Marlow

Brother

Bass-player
Skate-nutter
Girlfriend-dumper
Nickname-hater
Detention-maker
School-detester
Brother-puncher
Spot-grower.

Charlie Wrenn (10)
Spinfield School, Marlow

Hamster

Fur-licker
Stuffy-eater
Flea-finder
Loud-sleeper
Mind-sweeper
Goal-keeper
Heavy-leaper.

Thomas Harris (10) & Natalie Rump (11)
Spinfield School, Marlow

Boys!

Messy-eater,
Fast-runner,
Mind-freakers,
Rude-speakers,
Girl-fanciers,
Long-sleepers,
Poor-shoppers,
Frightful-fakers.

Bethany Ayres (10) & Cate Holmes (11)
Spinfield School, Marlow

My Cat

Mouse trapper
Milk lapper
Wild purrer
Argument stirrer
Toe picker
Rough licker
Loud eater
Lap heater
Fantastic hearer
Brave creature
Terrific bouncer
Wild pouncer
Fast runner
Tree stunner.

Alexandra Openshaw (10)
Spinfield School, Marlow

New York

Taxi-user
Statue-holder
Party-popper
Traffic-jammer
Factory-former
Subway-super
Liberty-praiser
Sky-scraper
Criss-crosser
Sharp-shooter.

Chris Byatt (10) & Jonathan Wilson (11)
Spinfield School, Marlow

Rabbit

Foot-kicker
Little-nibbler
Human-licker
Lettuce-muncher
Silly-jumper
Crazy-frolicker
Claw-catcher
Ear-slapper
Fur-hugger
Strange-runner
Frightened-hider
Sleepy-dreamer
Food-protector.

Oliver Connolly (11)
Spinfield School, Marlow

Girls

Brain creepers
Boy scarers
Mind freakers
Creepy glarers
Quick talkers
Animal lovers
Fashion admirers
Make-up adorers
Fancy dressers
Loud screamers.

Alex Roe (10)
Spinfield School, Marlow

Dog

Ball chaser
Doggy paddler
Cat hater
Ear scratcher
Attention seeker
Stick fetcher
Man lover
Food scoffer
Long sleeper
Flea itcher
Loud barker.

Greg Broughton (10)
Spinfield School, Marlow

Mum

Food-collector
Dish-washer
Meal maker
Lunch-packer
Dust-destroyer
Scarf-provider
Taxi-driver
School-worker
Literacy-reader
Fell-walker
Kind-smiler.

Stephanie Leake (10)
Spinfield School, Marlow

Cats

Huge-glarer
Carpet-tearer
Tree-leaper
Roof-creeper
Flesh-gnawer
Person-pawer
Mouse-disemboweler
Moon-howler
China-breaker
Fabric-raker
Selective-eater
Bird-beater.

Alice Bolton (10)
Spinfield School, Marlow

My Rabbit

Dark-dasher
Lean-leaper
Gradual-eater
Chubby-cuddlier
Fluffy-roller
Friendly-facer
Lazy-sleeper
Loud-snorer
Humorous-dreamer
Speedy-runner
Chief-bosser
Treat-taker
Mess-maker
Brown-eyed-creature.

Joanna Taylor (10)
Spinfield School, Marlow

My Kitten

Mouse-stalker
Vermin-grabber
Skunk-smeller
Plant-patter
Greedy-gobbler
Elder-beater
Crazy-clawer
Merry-maker.

Sophie Kemp (10)
Spinfield School, Marlow

A Puppy

Finger-nibbler
Deep-sleeper
Speed-sprinter
Leg-pawer
Human-adorer
High-hopper
Face-fondler.

Emily Ford (10)
Spinfield School, Marlow

Sister

Fantastic looker
Night clubber
A shoe shopper
Dazzling dater
Boy flirter
Disco lover
Hip hop dancer
Binge drinker
Hair styler.

Victoria Stiles (10)
Spinfield School, Marlow

The Whale That Swallowed The Ship

'Twas a stormy day
In the middle of the sea,
As pirates were on board their ship
Unknown to them a whale swam
Searching for his tea.

Up he popped and snapped their ship
And swallowed them happy as can be.

The ship was gone
The pirates were starving
Hoping they could live,
'Achoo!'
They came out with such a whizz.

They might have been stranded
But they gave a great cheer
Living on coconuts
They celebrated over beer!

Ben Rout (10)
Stanway Primary School, Colchester

A Whale Who Swallowed A Boat

'Twas a sunny day on the ocean
The white whale was swimming about,
While a sailing boat was looking for fish.

The white whale looked at the boat with the men on board,
And then the boat looked at the whale.
'Get the net!' shouted the captain.

And then the whale swam nearer the boat,
And then the whale swam through the net.
And then the net snapped in half.
The whale was so angry he ate the boat.

The white whale swam home,
And on the way he choked on the boat
And the whale spat out the boat.

Rosie Potter (10)
Stanway Primary School, Colchester

Alien Who Came To Earth!

Zooming through space,
Without any care,
The sky is dark and starry,
I'm nearly there!

I'd landed, I'd landed
Whoopee! Whoopee!
Oh no, what had I done?
A big crack is what I could see.

Quickly, quickly I tried to mend it
But it didn't work!
I got some glue out of my kit
And glued it back together.

I got in my ship,
Looking forward to a rest!
I was nearly home,
My family shouted out, 'You fixed the Earth,'
And, 'You're the best!'

Naomi Paige-Clark (11)
Stanway Primary School, Colchester

The Whale Who Swallowed A Ship

'Twas a cold and rainy day
A whale hungry in the sea
Trying to find something to eat
He came across a ship the size of a pea.

The big fish swam over to it
But the boat just sailed past
So the whale swam up and swallowed it whole
Down went the ship so fast.

They tried to escape but 'twas locked
They were in there for hours and the time went tick-tock.

Charlotte Jones (10)
Stanway Primary School, Colchester

The Whale That Swallowed A Ship

'Twas a bright summer's day,
A whale swam in the ocean blue,
Swimming around looking for food,
To find a ship and eat you and me.

At last he found a ship,
One with a big sail,
So they all got swallowed,
By that great big whale.

'Let us out!' the scared men shouted
But the whale just swam away,
'If we ever get out,' bellowed the men,
'This deadly whale will pay!'

A few days passed and the men were cold and hungry
The whale felt queasy and swam slow,
The mammal stopped and spat up the ship,
The men were fine and one called out, 'We must go!'

Lorna Mayne (10)
Stanway Primary School, Colchester

The Whale Who Swallowed A Ship

'Twas a beautiful sunny day,
When a big blue whale swam to look for food,
But a ship full of fish suddenly appeared,
Now the blue whale was in a good mood.

A sudden big splash sprung up,
As the tail crashed down in the sea,
Closer and closer the whale swam,
The sailor said, 'Why is it always me?'

The fish took one big bite,
And happy he'd be
He found a ship, a big ship too,
At last he'd had his tea.

Jessica Dunn (10)
Stanway Primary School, Colchester

The Whale Who Swallowed A Ship

'Twas a clear rainy day
And a whale in the sea,
Was starving hungry
But couldn't find its tea.

Then a ship came along,
Sailing right past
So the whale did follow,
Swimming quite fast.

The mammal ate the ship,
With one big crunch.
But 'twas too hollow to chew
So the whale couldn't munch.

2 hours later the ship escaped
With all men on board
Maud the whale met a male
And they got married behind swords.

Sheena Wooldridge (10)
Stanway Primary School, Colchester

The Whale Who Swallowed A Ship!

'Twas a beautiful summer's day
A ship was sailing across the deep blue sea
A huge grey whale was swimming without any care
Suddenly he appeared and the crew started to flee.

The whale did follow
But flipped his tail
And gave one swallow
Then he gave one wail.

Oh no, the ship was gone!
How did he do it without a doubt?
Well, he swallowed it whole
So I'd better watch out!

Emily Fisk (10)
Stanway Primary School, Colchester

The Whale Who Swallowed A Ship

'Twas a whale, a big blue whale, waiting for something to eat
His friends he wanted to race
And he wanted to beat
Here came a ship, one full of fish.

For him it was a perfect dish
A delicious cargo
A lovely one full of fish
Up flung his tail.

Suddenly, *crash, bang, thump!*
There was no longer a ship
He spat them onto the beach
Just like an orange pip
Crash, bang, thump, bump!

Chloe Veal (10)
Stanway Primary School, Colchester

The Whale That Swallowed A Ship

'Twas a fine sunny day,
When a great blue whale was hungry,
It felt like eating a ship,
As its tummy was extremely rumbly!

At last it found a vessel,
With a swishing big sail
And it swallowed it all in one,
Then everyone screamed, 'Help! A savage whale!'

Now there was no sign of the ship,
All that was left was the sail
And no one knows what happened to this ship,
That vessel that was swallowed by a whale!

Stephanie Allston (10)
Stanway Primary School, Colchester

The Alien Who Caused Mischief On Earth

'I'm nearly there, just a few minutes now,
I can see it, the big green ball!
I'm coming into land, here I go,
But I've go to be careful not to fall.'

Splash! 'Looks like I'm here,
Now I've got to find a clock.'
He took out his mischief maker,
And to stop the time he put on a lock.

While the time had stopped,
He switched lots of things around,
Then the alien put the clocks right,
The police came and he was found!

The chief alien, back in space,
Was sad to see him again,
So he sent down another alien,
To the peculiar world of men!

Hannah Coe (10)
Stanway Primary School, Colchester

The Whale Who Swallowed A Ship!

'Twas on a bright sunny day,
A ship was sailing in the ocean blue,
The passengers all safe and calm,
Including the old captain too.

Suddenly a dark, gloomy shadow,
With razor-sharp teeth,
Swallowed up the great white ship,
Some people on top swam down beneath.

The survivors stuck inside the whale,
All began to stink
But soon they were all eaten up,
At least that's what I think.

Sarah Kerry (9)
Stanway Primary School, Colchester

The Whale Who Swallowed A Ship

On the blue sea the whaling ship was sailing
And a whale was out for food all alone,
They saw each other combined and whined,
And only to hear was a whale's moan.

A net then fell in the deep blue sea,
And tangled up the whale
But to their surprise the fish escaped,
So that was a definite fail.

The whale became angry
And broke the ship in half.
All the pirates were scared,
And there was no cause to laugh.

The mammal began to starve
And ate the ship and men
But unlike lots of other ships,
They were never seen again.

Zoe Bull   (10)
Stanway Primary School, Colchester

The Whale Who Swallowed A Ship

A ship was sailing on a peaceful ocean
And men were climbing above the sea
Then the waves began to toss and smash
And men began to flee.

A fountain of water came flying out of the ocean
And then arose a whale.
It opened its mouth and the ship fell in
And then it splashed its tail.

The men inside were never seen again
Or the captain with the blue navy hat
Nor the ship with the oak planks
And the vessel's cat.

Joseph Gibbon   (10)
Stanway Primary School, Colchester

The Whale Who Swallowed A Ship

'Twas a hot sunny day
When we sailed the sea
We saw a great white whale
He was staring at me.

Then all of a sudden
He swallowed us whole
And we were whizzing down his throat
Like a football towards a goal.

My crew went mad
And dived into the waves
I was the only one left
I had to be brave.

Then out of nowhere
There came a gush of air
And I flew towards the beach
Without a care.

Scott Hadley (11)
Stanway Primary School, Colchester

The Alien Arrival

'Great, oh great, it's Earth at last, a giant green and blue ball.'
The alien arrived with a bash and a clang.
'Oh, the sea is like a great long wall.

The world is so busy with people, sea and land,
The city, yippee I'm nearly there,
Hurray, a hip rock band.

A lovely smelling rubbish tip,
Yippee I'm on my way.'
Tick-tock, it's time to go.
'Oh no, can't I stay?'

Charlotte Bellotti (10)
Stanway Primary School, Colchester

The Whale That Swallowed A Ship

'Twas a stormy day in the middle of the sea
Everything was calm so far
The pirates ate their tea in peace
Shouting, 'Ooh aah! Ooh aah!'

Unknown to them the whale swam below
Searching for his tea
He waited, he waited
But he was too hungry.

He noticed the ship
And with a tap
The boat quickly went snap
The first bit, his favourite, the tip.

Once the ship was down
The great mammal gave a frown
He had an itch and then a twitch
Achoo! Out popped the pirates, down, down, down.

Christian Stephens (10)
Stanway Primary School, Colchester

The Whale Who Swallowed A Ship

A ship was sailing across the ocean
When a storm arose and sent the ship off course
A whale came and swallowed them up
And in his stomach they found a corpse.

The ship crashed further into the fish
Until it reached the bottom of his belly
But one of the shipmates committed suicide
Because the whale swallowed their telly.

The whale started to shake
And up went the ship
The whale was sick
And the ship came out through his lips.

Dominic Harris (10)
Stanway Primary School, Colchester

A Whale That Swallowed A Ship!

'Twas a sunny ship journey with a crew of five men
And a captain of the seven seas who drank a lot of ale with them
But a dopey-looking crew member looked from the stern
He didn't tell captain
There was a mammal in front of them.

And in the Pacific Ocean a whale just 'gulped' them up
But the crew saw they were stuck
The captain said, 'While we are waiting let's clean the whale's muck!'
After two hours a man said, 'This foul job sucks!'

Then the whale mumbles,
'What's going on down there?
The crew has gone insane and are dancing like bears.'
One used a tooth like a loo
The ship was finally cracked in two.

But then three men were digested with very naughty thoughts
The other three were sneezed out with very happy thoughts
Then the men landed at Hawaii, life was very good
Until a lightning storm appeared and zapped the captain too!

Jonathan Lam (10)
Stanway Primary School, Colchester

The Alien That Visited Earth

'Twas a rainy and sunny, Earthly day
But unknown to humans an alien was there
He wanted to find a pot of gold.
So he followed a rainbow full of care.

For days he followed that rainbow
Till he reached the end of that rainbow
Then he decided,
'I'd better leave now. I'll go.'

Luke Allston (11)
Stanway Primary School, Colchester

The Whale That Swallowed A Ship

'Twas on a fine, sunny day
Dolphins were swimming without a care.
Then we heard a noise so quickly we sailed away,
We don't know where
But as we did a whale did follow
It came swimming closer
Our ship it was very hollow.

It would have broken it if he had crashed into the side
But he decided to swallow us instead
His belly was very wide
I nearly fell down dead.

After a couple of days he sicked us up
I couldn't believe we were out of there
I was home at last so I had some tea in my favourite cup
I don't know if anyone really cared.

Daisy Farthing (9)
Stanway Primary School, Colchester

Alien Mischief Maker

'Is that all it is, a blue and green blob?'
The alien was travelling, travelling to Earth.
Falling, falling down to Earth,
Landing on a lump of turf.

Everything started to go wrong
'Those children are in great woe!
I must help them, set them free,'
So the alien helped them to the greatest place to go.

When it was over, the police came
With a great big knock on the door
They found the alien, and sent him back
To the planet where the aliens said, 'Shut the floor!'

Katie Dobson (10)
Stanway Primary School, Colchester

What Is A Guitar Shop?

It is a boat on a calm, tranquil sea
Inside a sensor to catch a shark
At the far end several sharks hung up like clothes on a washing line
A set of stark teeth in all shapes and sizes like daggers drawn
A survival guide with a flesh-cutting survival knife
And fire like thorns on a rose
In the centre of the boat a counter with fish meat everywhere
And out of the tranquil sea fresh sharks circling.

Joe Bees (11)
Tany's Dell Community Primary School & Nursery, Harlow

What Is Highbury?

Red blurs everywhere you look
Crowds cheer when a goal goes in
Players run extremely fast, trying to get a gasp of air
The commentators shout as a team moves on to an attack
People play loud, heavy music
Others around the stadium look out from their windows
The ref blows the whistle and half-time is up.

Wesley Stephens (11)
Tany's Dell Community Primary School & Nursery, Harlow

The Spring Poem

It explodes on the dark landscape like a firework,
Light green and fluffy pink blossom bursting out of dark dead wood
Butterflies fluttering around like a sparkler on a cold winter's night.

Yasmin Hartley (10)
Tany's Dell Community Primary School & Nursery, Harlow

The Queen

With a golden, sparkly, shiny crown
Upon her hair short and brown
Her eyes brightening, glowing
Her pink lips are showing
A purple dress with silver balls
Pink shoes that are as flat as a wall
So kind and caring
With the people sharing.

Amina Begum Ali (10)
Tany's Dell Community Primary School & Nursery, Harlow

My Poem

The water crashing against the rocks like crashing cars
Sharp shark teeth shooting up from the water
Orange and rainbow fish swaying underneath the water,
Wet, watery mud
People swaying side to side
What is this poem about?

Jodie Hester (11)
Tany's Dell Community Primary School & Nursery, Harlow

What Is A Farmyard?

It's a mass of clashing colours and clanking engines.
It's a carnivorous kennel full of yapping dogs and screeching cats.
It's a filthy garage full of broken engines and punctured tyres.
It's a gungy sewer full of mould and goo.

Jasmine O'Brien (10)
Tany's Dell Community Primary School & Nursery, Harlow

The Princess

Long, shiny, blonde hair
Blue, sparkling eyes
Smooth, peach lips
Cheeks like red roses.
A beautiful, pink rose dress
She moves gracefully.
Pointed toes like a ballerina
She smells like a peach rose
Her smile is so sweet
Blinking slowly like a butterfly
Her heart pounds
She kisses the prince
Falling in love
Forever together.

Angelle Essuman (11)
Tany's Dell Community Primary School & Nursery, Harlow

My Bedroom

I dream of a bedroom as pink as icing on a doughnut
I dream of a bed as comfortable as cottonwool clouds
I dream of pillows like candyfloss from the fair
I dream of 10,000 DVDs to keep me up all night
I dream of music to rattle my bedroom like a rock concert
I dream of windows as big as plasma screens
Too see the calm world beyond.

Emily Bennett (11)
Tany's Dell Community Primary School & Nursery, Harlow

What Is A Haunted Mansion?

A haunted mansion is a horrifying dungeon
Creaking in the floorboards like ancient old ladies' knees
Rattles in the bedroom like snakes in a desert.

Unsuspecting eyes flicker like flashes of a photograph
Ice steps twist and turn up endless passages
Lights disappear like magical magicians disappearing off a stage.

Creepy-crawlies scattering across cracks in the floorboards
Like a black cat scurrying along a dark alleyway,
Suits of armour shine and follow your step like a lonely black shadow.

What is a haunted mansion?
It's a nightmare in the night!

Katie Henderson (11)
Tany's Dell Community Primary School & Nursery, Harlow

Siberian Tiger

Her nose is like
A shiny, black, smooth pebble
Blue eyes sparkling
Like the powder-blue sky
Her chin is as soft
As a white fluffy cushion
As sweet as a teddy bear
She is ready to pounce
Staring at prey
Making her family so happy
They're not hungry anymore.

Paige Crossfield (11)
Tany's Dell Community Primary School & Nursery, Harlow

The Match

I dribble the football
Round the players like Henry.

As I kick the football
Like a meteorite flying in space.

The glowing white ball
Cushions into the back of the net.

The cheers echo like
Someone shouting in a huge tunnel.

Playing on the huge football pitch.

George Stokes (10)
Tany's Dell Community Primary School & Nursery, Harlow

Lords

White, bright ghosts walking to the crease
People cheering like lions waiting for meat
Chants, cheers, cries all around.
The bright red slashes on their white trousers look like blood.
When the batsman slogs the ball you can hear the clonk
As it whistles through the air and lands with a *thud*
On the lush green outfield.

Jonathon Whitnall (11)
Tany's Dell Community Primary School & Nursery, Harlow

Manchester Stadium

Inside the stadium it holds 96 thousand people
When the match starts with Man U kicking the ball to start the match
Arsenal get fired up for the big game
It will be the best test in the world.
A bundle of people cheering as the ball goes into the net
Like a rocket zooming past.

Jamie Emmerman (11)
Tany's Dell Community Primary School & Nursery, Harlow

The Sea

A swirl of sapphire with sequins whirling around her,
Mountains of blue crashing against her wimple of gravel
A layer of golden beneath the beautiful blue,
Hurdles of tiny fish like a wiggling rainbow
Bushes of lush green in her golden quilt
People like giants with flippers and masks on the black silk bodies
Squeaking silver creatures jumping their way through the blue
Enormous boat bobbing in her sparkle.
Tangles of net catching all the beloved fish
Yellow moon shapes whizzing through her.
Creatures with snapping teeth like thorns
A king of the water with a sprinkle coming out of his head
Like a trickle of water, a fearless tail wagging down into the sea.

Sophie Natynczyk (10)
Tany's Dell Community Primary School & Nursery, Harlow

The Good Fairy

She has lovely golden hair
Her cheeks are like roses
A dress like the golden sun
Shoes like glass slippers
Her wings are like a stained glass window
She has a sparkling wand
Her hair is as curly as Goldilocks'
Her lips are like pink roses
Her wand is like a star
Flying through the sky
Bringing magic to the children
As she's passing them by.

Katie Green (10)
Tany's Dell Community Primary School & Nursery, Harlow

What Is A Castle?

A castle is a place where medieval soldiers fight for their lives
A place like a haunted mansion
Deserted and taken over by ghosts and spirits,
Souls that once lived through a bloodbath.
In human bodies that are now long gone.
Slashes of bloodstains against the side of the wall
When you touch, still warm
But not a living soldier in sight,
Corpses everywhere, rotting away each second.
That is not the worst yet,
You can see swords from combat
That have been thrust into the hell-born men
When you kick open the door, with a feeling of loneliness
Just remember, don't be afraid.
When you see an empty throne with a crown on top,
Hear the wind howling,
See the lanterns glimmering with a dim light . . . gone!
There is no light, you can't see a thing, face it, you're lost
There is no way out without light
But then you wake up.
And it's all just a nightmare.
Hang on, where is everyone?

Jack Wheeler (10)
Tany's Dell Community Primary School & Nursery, Harlow

The Motorbike

With his glistening coat on he runs down the hill
He purrs and purrs but carries on running
Getting into his stride he jumps over ramps
As big and merciless as bloodthirsty trolls
He rolls up the driveway then slowly continues
And, purring no more, the motorbike stops.

Jack Smith (10)
Tany's Dell Community Primary School & Nursery, Harlow

River To The Sea

A fierce wind blew me from my branch
I plummeted straight down; I had no chance,
I plunged through the water and smote the riverbed,
For a moment I thought I would drown and be dead,
But no! I floated up to the surface
On the way I saw a couple of silver fish,
I started my journey, getting faster and faster
I realised the water was getting lighter and lighter.
The sky-blue river was really rushing now
I crashed against a rock, my head was spinning round and round
I was in a cycloning whirl of rapids,
(Never ever try this at home, kids!)
Suddenly I felt a tremendous drop
Splash! I fell down a waterfall, my head was going to pop
The current of the river carried me out to the sea
I could hear the seagulls and smell the salt
On the beach I could see children and adults,
I rolled over to relieve my remaining sodden leaves
By sticking them up in the great ocean breeze.

Oskar Thomas (10)
West Walton Community Primary School, Wisbech

Pistols In My Pocket

I wish I were a pirate,
Sailing in my ship.
My pistols in my pockets,
My sword by my hip.
The sea smell in the air,
Sharks circling me.
I let the anchor down and yanked it back up,
To find I had the catch of the day.

Callum Pitcher (11)
West Walton Community Primary School, Wisbech

The Seaside

Waves roaring
Sunshine pouring
Cliffs falling
Seagulls calling
What else can you hear?

Silver fish smelling
Chip shop selling
Sea salt compelling
Anything else you can smell?

Children playing
Adults laying
Pensioners saying
Anything else you can see?

Joyful feelings
Happy feelings
Excited feelings
What else can you feel?

Charlotte Sear (11)
West Walton Community Primary School, Wisbech

Sea Storm

Sloshing and hurtling and stabbing
Interrupting and troubling and stammering
Flaxen and pearly and ultramarine
Sneakily and contented and malicious
Salty and malty and sandy.
It can smell the candy
Watching and waiting and inflating
And creating this unhesitating
Wave.

Caitlin Thorpe (10)
West Walton Community Primary School, Wisbech

The Sea, Mistress To All

She's a slow mover to start
Then she whips the seabed apart
She has the most melodic sound
That'll sweep you off the golden ground
Her movements like an aqua angel rippling throughout Heaven
You'll feel her dove-like waves glide past you
When you do you'll be in Heaven
Peace be with you.

The smell is fresh it's one of a kind
The sound will echo in your mind
The sight is miraculous, simply divine
I wish the whole sea; I could keep to be mine.

James Gifford (10)
West Walton Community Primary School, Wisbech

Winter Beach

A winter beach
Not a pleasant place to be
Wind crashing, cliffs smashing
Like a rhino in the sea.

A winter beach
Not a pleasant feeling in the air,
Rotting fish, stomach curdling
Smells get tangled in your hair.

A winter beach,
Not a pleasant place to be,
So go take a dip
And you will see!

Lorna Deller (10)
West Walton Community Primary School, Wisbech

Senses Of The Sea

Children playing,
People saying,
These are the sights of the sea.

Waves eroding,
People moaning,
These are the sounds of the sea.

Mind changing,
People rearranging,
These are the affects of the sea.

Salt smell,
All being well,
These are the smells of the sea.

Laura Tilney (10)
West Walton Community Primary School, Wisbech

Night-Time Beach

The beach at night is a ghastly place,
Waves like rearing horses,
Wind like a cutting knife,
See lightning flashing,
Rain will come dashing,
The heavens are scowling,
Hear thunder growling
A storm has suddenly come on!

Feel the tensions rise,
Waves come crashing by,
Wind like a girl's cry,
Have you been to the beach at night?

Maise Hunns (11)
West Walton Community Primary School, Wisbech

The Seaside

Waves crashing, crashing
Water swishing, swishing
Children shouting, shouting
Seagulls squawk, squawk
Parents always silent
That's what I can hear
Hot dogs sizzling, sizzling
Chips frying, frying
Crisps crunching, crunching
That's what I can taste
Lifeguards watching
Children swimming
Parents bathing
Boats sailing
People walking
That's what I can see.

Christopher Vick (10)
West Walton Community Primary School, Wisbech

The Sea And Its Friends

Sea goes crashing
Straight rocks smashing,
Waves clatter madly,
Tearing cliffs badly.

White horse splashes
Hear the clashes
Waves clawing beaches
At all features.

Kelsey McKenna (10)
West Walton Community Primary School, Wisbech

At The Beach

At the beach I hear . . .
Waves rumbling
Seagulls screeching
Sand crumbling,
Children cheering
I hear all these at the beach.

At the beach I see . . .
People swimming,
Coastguards watching,
Grannies paddling,
Ladies visiting
I see all this at the beach.

At the beach I feel . . .
Mood changing
Life rearranging
Mind lifting
Stress leaving,
I feel all this at the beach.

At the beach I smell . . .
Chips cooking,
Hot dogs burning,
Doughnuts baking,
Burgers cooling,
I smell all this at the beach.

Emma Rogers (10)
West Walton Community Primary School, Wisbech

Roaring Thunder

How many pebbles make a seabed?
How many waves make a sea?
How many shells make a shore?
How many tides to erode the cliffs?

How many corals make a reef?
How many reefs make an underwater jungle?
How many waves to destroy a cliff?
How many jellyfish in the sea?

How many rocks make a cliff?
How many people to pollute the sea?
How much seaweed to fill the sea?
How much oil to kill the fishes?

Who knows?
Not me!

Sam Melton (10)
West Walton Community Primary School, Wisbech

The Coast

Sea bends and sways like motorways
Cliffs are boring, they're never moving
But they're a good view to start the morning
I feel the smooth sand tickling my feet
I envision the crabs walking along the sand.

Shattered shells scattered all around
I even sink into the sand
I smell the salt from the sea
And the taste of the salt is next
I hear the children laughing
I see the children building sandcastles
How much better can the beach be?

Paul Whyatt (11)
West Walton Community Primary School, Wisbech

What Can You Feel?

What can you feel?
I can feel the cold breeze hitting my face,
I can feel the wind rushing through my hair,
I can feel the waves crashing against my body pushing me back.

What can you see?
I can see the waves crashing against my body,
I can see the seagulls flying round the sea,
I can see the wind blowing bits of paper round and round my feet.

What can you smell?
I can smell fish and chips cooking as people are eating them,
I can smell the fresh air as the sea crashes beneath my feet,
I can smell the salt in the sea.

What can you hear?
I can hear children laughing as they tell jokes,
I can hear waves crashing against the cliffs.
I can hear people talking about their day.

What can you taste?
I can taste fish and chips as I put them in my mouth
I can taste the fresh air as I breathe
I can taste the salt from the chips.

Alice Edwards (11)
West Walton Community Primary School, Wisbech

The Beach

Looks fabulous,
Golden grains,
Seashore shells,
Umbrellas held.

Seaside paddle,
Salty, freezing sea,
Boats in the distance
Are water resistant.

Bethany Brightey (10)
West Walton Community Primary School, Wisbech

The Tide

The tide went out
Dead fish were everywhere
Fishing men collected the fish
People were going through the leaf-green path
On the beach the fire-red sun
Everywhere the waves hit the cliff like a thunderstorm
Rocks fall with a crack and crash and smash.
The sapphire sea washes away the electric sand
Sandcastles here, sandcastles there, the shells everywhere
Buckets and spades, holes in the ground
People in the sea, lifeguards eating a cookie
It is late, the tide is coming in
The sandcastles are being washed away.

Jonathan Thompson (10)
West Walton Community Primary School, Wisbech

Beach Poem

The rippling of the rock pools
The crashing of the waves
The swimming of the dolphins
The underwater caves.

The screeching of the seagulls
The texture of the sand
The height of the cliffs
Really is grand.

The speed of the jet-ski
The smell of the ice cream
The sliminess of the seaweed
All this is at the beach.

Bethany Smith (11)
West Walton Community Primary School, Wisbech

Coastline

I went down to see the sea today
The sand is a gorgeous pinkish-yellow
There are thousands of striped shells scattered everywhere
I see a beautiful sea today.

I went down to see the sea today
The electric sea laps the shore
As the cliffs slowly crumble away
I see a beautiful sea today.

I went down to see the sea today
Feeling the sand between my toes
Smelling the sea salt
I see a beautiful sea today.

Aaron Gosling (11)
West Walton Community Primary School, Wisbech

I Wish I Were A Pirate

I wish I were a pirate
Sailing on my boat,
With the gentle waves,
Lapping at the sides,
Pistol in my pocket,
I smell the salty air,
Hear the waves crashing,
Dashing, all I see is
A storm looking me
Straight in the eye,
I can taste the rain,
I feel the boat,
Going side to side.

Liam Follen (10)
West Walton Community Primary School, Wisbech

The Sea

Waves crashing madly
Rocks breaking badly.

The sea's hidden powers
Destroying kids' towers.

I swam under the sea
It was beautiful as can be.

James Brazil (10)
West Walton Community Primary School, Wisbech

I Wish

I wish I could see her just under the sea
Then it will be just her and me
I wish I could see her lovely tail
I wish I could see her with her fair hair
I wish I could hear her sing
Oh I wish I could be a mermaid.

Rebecca Crane (11)
West Walton Community Primary School, Wisbech

Mermaid

I wish I could see her again.
I wish I could hear her again with her lovely tail.
I wish I could feel her again with her lovely gold hair and silky tail.
I wish I could smell the salted sea
I could taste the splash of gold on the sand and sea.

Nicole Young (10)
West Walton Community Primary School, Wisbech

The Beach

I see rapid waves
I see gradual waves
I see children running around
I see adults trying to get a tan
I see grannies and grandads walking in and out
I see the aqua sea
I see the blazing sand.

I hear the waves rushing
I hear the children laughing
I hear the adults talking.

I feel the blazing sand
I feel the aqua sea.

I smell the seaweed
I smell the salt.

I taste the salt in the sea
I taste the seaweed
I taste the water.

Robert Brooks (10)
West Walton Community Primary School, Wisbech